Leading Beyond the Desk: My Lessons from the Real World of Leadership

OrangeBooks Publication

1st Floor, Rajhans Arcade, Mall Road, Kohka, Bhilai, Chhattisgarh 490020

Website: **www.orangebooks.in**

First Edition, 2025

ISBN: 978-93-7426-936-7

Price: Rs. 395.00

Printed in India

LEADING BEYOND THE DESK

MY LESSONS FROM THE REAL WORLD OF LEADERSHIP

Building Teams, Scaling Innovation, and Leading Across Cultures

LIYAKHAT ALI KHAN

OrangeBooks Publication
www.orangebooks.in

Dedication

To my family, mentors, and all the leaders who inspired me to write this book. Special mention to:

1. Mr. Vikas Bawa (Previously Manager – Interiors @ Mahindra & Mahindra Ltd.)
2. Mr. Gilles Bysweski (Previously CTO @ TACO Faurecia Design Center Ltd)
3. Mr. Vinayak Shendkar (Previously Project Manager @ TACO Faurecia Design Center Ltd.)
4. Mr. Torsten Meier (Previously Vice President @ Mercedes Benz R&D India)
5. All my team members at TACO Faurecia, Mercedes Benz R&D India & Daimler Truck Innovation Center India who I had the opportunity to work along & lead

All of the above, I had the opportunity to observe, adapt and learn through our interactions. You all have been a very strong influence in my personal leadership journey. Thank you!

Foreword

Leadership is not a title or a position—it's a way of being, a commitment to serving others while pursuing a shared vision. In my 1.5 decades of studying and practicing leadership, I've observed that the most effective leaders are those who understand this fundamental truth.

When Liyakhat Ali Khan asked me to write the foreword for this book, I was surprised but honoured. Having known Liyakhat for several years and been a first-hand witness in his professional journey in leadership, I knew this would be a valuable contribution to the field. What you hold in your hands is not merely theoretical knowledge, but practical wisdom earned through real-world experience.

This book addresses the critical challenges facing today's leaders: building trust in an age of scepticism, inspiring teams in times of uncertainty, and maintaining authenticity while navigating complex organizational dynamics. Liyakhat Ali Khan tackles these challenges with clarity, honesty, and actionable insights.

What sets this work apart is its emphasis on authentic leadership—the kind that comes from knowing yourself deeply and leading from that place of truth. Too many leadership books offer formulaic solutions that ignore the human element. This book recognizes that effective leadership is deeply personal and requires continuous self-reflection and growth. Whether you're a seasoned executive, an emerging leader, or someone aspiring to make a greater impact, you'll find valuable lessons in these pages. The principles shared here are timeless, yet their application is remarkably relevant to our current moment.

I encourage you to read this book not as a passive observer, but as an active participant in your own leadership development. Take notes, reflect on the questions posed, and most importantly, apply what you learn. The world needs authentic leaders now more than ever. Thank you for taking this important step in your leadership journey.

- Azma Liyakhat, Wife and Homemaker

Pune, 2025

Preface

I never set out to write a book about leadership. Like many leaders, I stumbled into my first leadership role with more enthusiasm than expertise, learning through trial and error, making mistakes, and gradually discovering what it meant to truly lead others.

This book was born from those experiences—the late nights questioning decisions, the conversations that changed my perspective, the failures that taught me more than any success ever could, and the profound privilege of watching people grow and achieve things they never thought possible.

Over the years, I've had the opportunity to lead teams in various contexts, to study leadership formally and informally, and to observe exceptional leaders up close. What struck me most was the gap between what leadership books promised and what leadership actually required. So many books offered neat frameworks and inspirational stories, but few addressed the messy reality of leading real people through real challenges.

This book is my attempt to bridge that gap. It's written for the leader who wants more than platitudes and quick fixes—for someone who understands that authentic leadership is a journey of continuous learning and growth.

You'll find here a blend of personal stories, hands on approaches, and practical tools. Some chapters will resonate immediately; others may become more relevant as your leadership journey unfolds. My hope is that you'll return to this book at different stages of your career and find new insights each time.

A few notes about how to use this book: First, leadership is not one-size-fits-all. Take what resonates and adapt it to your context. Second, the reflection questions at the end of each chapter are not mere exercises—they're invitations to do the deeper work of self-awareness that authentic leadership requires. Third, leadership is learned through action. Reading this book is a start, but the real learning happens when you apply these principles in your daily work, but most importantly find your own way.

I want to acknowledge that leadership can feel lonely. My hope is that in these pages, you'll find a companion for your journey—someone who understands the challenges you face and believes deeply in your capacity to lead with authenticity and impact.

Thank you for investing your time and attention in becoming a better leader. The work you do matters more than you know.

- Liyakhat Ali Khan

Pune, 2025

Introduction

My attempt to bring out real-world leadership from an engineer's lens — blending technical rigor, emotional intelligence, and personal evolution. As a technical person one of the challenges in transitioning into a good Leader — the journey maybe hard on a person as the attributes which have defined your success and worked in your favour do not proportionately translate in your leadership role. My attempt is to share my experiences with not only technical individuals but anyone who faces the challenge why it worked when you were running solo but the same approaches are not working when you are a leader.

Leadership is not a designation—it is a responsibility that demands courage, empathy, and consistency. This book brings together reflections, real-life experiences, and insights gathered through two decades of leading engineering teams, navigating corporate systems, and building cultures of trust. It captures the lessons learned in the field, not from textbooks. I hope that I can bring a difference through my experiences which I have shared in this book to upcoming, and existing leader's.

Table of Contents

Part – III
Leading in the Modern World

Part – IV
Inner Leadership: Mindset & Reflection

Part – V
Organizational Leadership & Culture

Part – VI
Personal Leadership Lessons

Part – VII
Closing Reflections

Part – I

Foundations of Leadership

01

Daring to Lead

"The true mark of a leader is the willingness to stick with a bold course of action – an unconventional business strategy, a unique product-development roadmap, a controversial marketing campaign – even as the rest of the world wonders why you're not marching in step with the status quo."

— Bill Taylor

(Source: https://quotefancy.com/quote/1710129/Bill-Taylor-The-true-mark-of-a-leader-is-the-willingness-to-stick-with-a-bold-course-of)

Who Dares?

Leadership is not a title hanging on an office door or a seat at the head of the table. It is an audacious choice—a deliberate act of courage that echoes through every decision, every relationship, and every moment of vulnerability we choose to embrace.

A leader is someone who dares to dream. Not the small, comfortable dreams that fit safely within the boundaries of what already exists, but the boundless visions that stretch possibility itself. This person looks at the world not as it is, but as it could be—and then has the temerity to invite others into that vision, to build it together.

A leader is someone who dares to lead from the front. They do not ask their teams to walk paths they haven't walked themselves. They do not hide behind hierarchy or delegate away the hardest parts. They roll up their sleeves, they take the first step, and they show through their own actions what commitment truly looks like. They understand that the power of leadership multiplies when people see it embodied, not merely commanded.

A leader is someone who dares to respect the human being regardless of rank. Whether you are the newest intern or the most senior executive, a true leader meets you with the same level of dignity, the same attentiveness, the same regard for your voice. They flatten the invisible walls that hierarchies build. They understand that insight, courage, and wisdom do not flow in only one direction—they emerge from everywhere, and the leader who listens discovers more than the leader who merely speaks.

A leader is someone who dares to risk it all when the moment demands it. This is not recklessness. This is the clarity to recognize when the stakes have risen beyond the comfortable, when playing it safe has become the greater risk. In those rare, crystalline moments, the true leader stands firm, places their conviction on the line, and moves forward even when the outcome is uncertain. This is where courage separates leadership from management.

A leader is someone who dares to take the fall. When things fail—and they will—this person does not scramble to assign blame or distance themselves from the wreckage. They step forward and own it. They bear the weight of responsibility. And then, in the same breath, they shield their team from unnecessary criticism and push them forward into the successes that follow. They understand that this is the bargain of leadership: you absorb the failures so your people can confidently attempt the next brave thing.

A leader is someone who dares to listen even when they've done nothing wrong. Their team member arrives carrying the weight of a personal crisis or a bad day or a confidence that has been shaken. The leader's first instinct is not to defend themselves or explain why it isn't their fault. Instead, they create space for that person to be heard. They offer their presence as an anchor in the storm. They recognize that humanity does not wait for perfect circumstances, and that sometimes the greatest act of leadership is simply showing up for someone when they need it most.

A leader is someone who dares to be the North Star in darkness. When uncertainty clouds the vision, when fear whispers that the path forward is unclear, the leader does not succumb to the panic around them. Instead, they become fixed and luminous—a constant point of reference that helps others navigate through the night. This requires not that they have all the answers, but that they have unwavering clarity about the direction, the values, and the purpose worth moving toward.

To Lead

There is a quiet moment that comes to all who choose to lead—a moment when the world is still, and you are left alone with the weight of what you carry and the trust that has been placed in your hands. In that moment, you understand that leadership is less about knowing the answers and more about having the grace to live the questions alongside those who follow.

To lead is to accept that you will be misunderstood. That you will fail. That there will be nights when you lie awake, wondering if you made the right choice, if you should have done more, spoken differently, dared further. And yet, you rise the next morning and do it all again—not because you are certain, but because uncertainty has never been an excuse for silence or retreat.

Leadership is the art of holding two truths at once: that you are flawed and human, and that this does not disqualify you from serving something greater than yourself. It is found in the spaces between what we are and what we aspire to be. It lives in the courage to remain vulnerable even as you provide strength to others. It breathes in the acknowledgment that the journey matters far more than the destination.

To lead is to dare. And to dare is to truly live—not safely tucked away in the known, but reaching toward something that transforms both the leader and the led. It is the most beautiful, terrifying, and sacred responsibility we can ever accept.

02

The Hidden Leverage - Maturity as a Leadership Multiplier

My Leadership Mantra: Work on Maturity First.

As a team lead, you would benefit much more if the individual in your team you are dealing with is more sorted. The challenge most of the time is to make your people understand that it is okay to think about yourself, but always keep the other perspective in mind—the organization, your peers, your superiors, your suppliers. This comes very naturally to you, perhaps because of your personality or because of your years of experience, which has given you the maturity to manage the outcome of transactions and events. Here, maturity is the key word.

Over the years, my learning is this: to manage a team effectively, working on the maturity of your team members will take care of 50% of all your challenges. Now that's a big claim, but it is what it is. I have no statistics to hold up my argument, but over the years this has definitely given me the necessary confidence that when you work on an individual's ability to be more mature in their approach, they become a better worker by being smarter, more solution-oriented—rather than a complainer. Most importantly, they become a better prepared individual to absorb, reflect, and project themselves forward.

The challenge is overcoming the barriers of all individual personas and the embedded, misdirected values and principles that people may have become used to throughout their careers. These have led to a development of maturity that, while physically and age-wise appears adult, emotionally seems to be lagging in miles. As a team lead, your task is to pass on and maintain the values and principles necessary to develop the right emotional maturity in your team members—an acceptable social construct in the world we live in—and ensure they own and are accountable for their actions.

As Jim Rohn said, "Maturity is the ability to reap without apology and not complain when things don't go well." True maturity means owning your outcomes—celebrating your wins without excuse-making, and accepting your failures without blame-shifting. It means being solution-oriented rather than complaint-driven. It means preparing yourself to absorb feedback, reflect on it, and project yourself forward differently.

The Goal-Setting Mirror: Where Maturity Reveals Itself

Goal-setting season offers a perfect window into the maturity level of your team. Let me share how this typically unfolds.

At the beginning of the year, I explain to my team that goal-setting is a contract for the year—a clear agreement with defined success criteria and ratings proportional to results. I ask them to review each measure carefully before committing. I create space for disagreement and invite them to register alternative measures during this window. I establish that progress will be tracked throughout the year, not compressed into a final review. I ensure every goal has visible checkpoints and milestones. The framework is clear. The expectations are transparent. The conversation is open.

Yet, year after year, I observe the same pattern: team members focus intensively on their core deliverable—the headline responsibility in their job description—while neglecting the broader goals necessary for team and organizational objectives. These secondary goals are often just as important, yet they receive minimal attention. When review time arrives and performance falls short, frustration emerges. "Why wasn't I rated higher? Why wasn't this recognized?"

This moment is revealing. It exposes the exact point where maturity breaks down.

Here is what immaturity looks like in this context: a person fails to deliver on clearly defined commitments, then expresses discontent about being held accountable to those exact commitments. They resist the feedback. They question the evaluator's fairness. They do not accept that their failure to deliver contributed to their results. They do not pause to reflect on where they went wrong.

Here is what maturity looks like: a person acknowledges where they fell short. They take responsibility. They ask themselves difficult questions. They commit to a different approach. They understand that performance outcomes are proportional to effort invested, and they own that equation.

This is not about perfection. This is about the willingness to stop, reflect, and respond—rather than react, blame, and repeat.

Emotional Maturity vs. Organizational Maturity

These two dimensions work together, but they are distinct, and understanding the difference is crucial for a leader.

Emotional maturity is your ability to manage yourself. It is about understanding your emotions, accepting them, and responding consciously rather than being controlled by them. It is understanding your vulnerability without letting it paralyze you. It is the capacity to fail, get back up, and try again—not once, but as many times as necessary. It is owning your mistakes because the truth matters more than your ego. As Jamal Crawford said, "It takes a certain level of maturity to get hit and get knocked down and get back up."

Organizational maturity is your ability to think beyond yourself. It is considering the implications of your actions on your peers, your team, your department, your organization. It is understanding that you are part of a system, and your behaviour affects that system. It is accepting that sometimes the right thing to do serves the collective interest rather than your personal convenience. It is having a growth mindset that sees failure as information, not condemnation.

Here is where it gets interesting: someone can be emotionally mature but organizationally immature. They handle their own emotions well, bounce back from setbacks, own their mistakes—but they still only think about themselves. They lack perspective on how their actions ripple outward.

Conversely, someone can appear organizationally savvy—they say the right things, they seem to understand the bigger picture—but they are emotionally fragile. When things don't go perfectly, when they face criticism, when they encounter obstacles, they crumble.

The highest performing team members have developed both dimensions. They understand themselves (emotional maturity) AND they understand their place in the larger ecosystem (organizational maturity).

The Path Forward

As a leader, your work is to cultivate both dimensions in your team. This requires:

- **Open communication and authentic feedback.** Tell your team members what you observe about their patterns and behaviours. Be real, even when it's uncomfortable. Share your own experiences—the mistakes you've made, how you've grown, what you've learned.
- **A growth mindset culture.** Team members get cornered by their failures and become reluctant to move on. As a leader, you must actively fight against this. Encourage them to stand immediately after they fall, to restart as many times as necessary. Reframe failure as data, not destiny.
- **Vulnerability as a leadership strength.** Help your team understand that it is not necessary to be brave all the time. Being strong enough to acknowledge vulnerability, to ask for guidance, to admit when you don't know something—this actually accelerates maturity.
- **Accountability as a gift, not a punishment.** Create an environment where owning mistakes is rewarded as much as celebrating wins. When someone comes forward and says, "I

missed the mark on this goal because I didn't prioritize it," that is an act of maturity. Honor it. Build on it.

The reality is this: you will encounter diverse personalities. Some will respond quickly to your efforts to build maturity. Others will resist. Some will be open to change; others will wait for external forces to solve their problems, never taking responsibility for their own development. There is no master key that unlocks every person. But here is what I have learned: even an incremental shift in how one person approaches their work, their relationships, and their challenges creates a multiplier effect. That person becomes a carrier of maturity. They influence others. They model a different way of being. Over time, they become a better engineer, a more reliable colleague, and potentially, a future leader who passes maturity forward to the next generation. This is the true multiplier. Not management systems or performance metrics, though those matter. But the quiet, patient, persistent work of helping human beings become more mature versions of themselves. That is where real leadership lives.

03

Technical Brilliance ≠ Leadership

The Promotion Trap

Every organization does it. When they need a leader, they look to their best performer. The engineer who writes flawless code. The designer who creates solutions that are not just functional, but beautiful. The analyst who spots patterns no one else can see. The salesman who closes deals consistently. The natural instinct is to promote them, to reward their excellence, to move them up the ladder. It feels right. It feels earned. It feels like a natural next step. But it is one of the most common mistakes organizations make. Because technical brilliance and leadership are not the same thing. They are not even on the same continuum. You cannot simply take someone who is exceptional at their craft and assume they will be exceptional at leading people. The skills that make you outstanding at your job do not translate automatically into the skills required to lead others. A great engineer might write flawless code, but can they inspire a junior developer who has lost confidence? A skilled designer might create beautiful, user-centric solutions, but can they hold space for a team member who is struggling? A sharp analyst might spot patterns no one else can, but can they communicate that insight in a way that brings a diverse team along? Leadership is a different game altogether.

The Three Pillars Leadership Demands

Leadership requires three things that technical brilliance does not.

- **First, empathy.** This is the ability to step into another person's world, to understand their motivations, their fears, their challenges, their aspirations. It is not enough to see what someone is doing wrong. You must understand why they are doing it. You must care enough to ask. Empathy is emotional intelligence in action—it is the antidote to the assumption that everyone thinks and operates the way you do.
- **Second, communication.** Technical brilliance can sometimes exist in isolation. A brilliant mind working alone can produce magnificent results. But leadership cannot exist in isolation. Leadership is the art of aligning diverse individuals—with different backgrounds, different thinking styles, different motivations—around a shared vision. This requires the ability to translate complexity into clarity, to listen more than you speak, to invite perspective rather than impose it. It requires saying the same thing in different ways until it lands, not because people aren't smart enough to understand, but because communication is fundamentally about connection, not transmission.
- **Third, inspiration.** A brilliant individual unlocks potential in themselves. A brilliant leader unlocks potential in others. This is the fundamental difference. Inspiration is not motivation—you cannot motivate someone else directly. But you can create the conditions where they motivate themselves. You can show them possibilities they hadn't considered. You can believe in them when they don't believe in themselves. You can help them see that their struggle is temporary, their growth is possible, their contribution matters. This is what transforms a team from a collection of individuals into a force.

The Jack Ma Principle

Consider Jack Ma, founder of Alibaba. By most measures, he was not a technical genius. He did not build the technology himself. He was not a programmer, an architect, or a systems engineer. He could not have written the code that powers Alibaba's ecosystem. Yet he transformed a company and changed the landscape of e-commerce in China and beyond.

How? Because his genius was not technical—it was human. He understood what people wanted before they knew it themselves. He could articulate a vision so compelling that thousands of talented engineers, designers, and entrepreneurs wanted to build it with him. He fostered a culture of empathy and collaboration. He created an environment where people didn't just do their jobs—they believed in something bigger.

His leadership wasn't about knowing more. It was about bringing out more in others. It was about seeing potential in people and creating space for that potential to flourish.

This is the principle that separates technical excellence from leadership excellence.

The Cost of Promotion Without Leadership Skills

I have seen it happen many times. A top performer gets promoted to manager. On paper, it makes sense. They've proven they can execute. They understand the work. The organization sees a seamless transition.

But then something shifts.

Instead of lifting the team, they become frustrated. They cannot understand why their team members don't see what they see, don't execute as quickly as they would, don't have the same instinctive mastery. So, they micromanage. They take work back. They become the bottleneck they were meant to replace. Or they burn out, trying to do their job and the team's job simultaneously, unable to let go of the work they were excellent at.

The result is a cascade of consequences:

- The individual loses confidence. They came in as the star and ended up feeling like a failure.
- The team loses morale. They feel untrusted, unheard, or overshadowed by someone who won't step back.

- The organization loses momentum. The role that should have freed up the brilliant individual to lead instead traps them in a cycle of frustration.
- Talent walks. Good people don't stay with managers who make them feel small.

A promotion without leadership skills isn't a reward. It's a setup for failure. For everyone involved.

The Organizations That Get It Right

The best organizations have learned this lesson. They don't assume that technical excellence automatically qualifies someone for leadership. Instead, they invest intentionally in the development of their future leaders.

- They offer leadership development programs.
- They create mentorship relationships where emerging leaders learn from experienced ones.
- They invest in emotional intelligence training—not as a nice-to-have, but as a core competency.
- They create space for people to develop leadership muscles before they are thrown into the deep end.
- Most importantly, they communicate clearly: **Promotion is not just about what you've done. It's about who you are becoming and who you choose to serve.**

This reframes leadership. It is not a reward for being the best at your job. It is a calling to bring out the best in others. It is not a trophy for individual excellence. It is a responsibility to steward people and culture. It is not a destination. It is a fundamental shift in how you think about your role in the world.

My Personal Mantra

In my leadership journey, I have learned this: **Leadership isn't about being the best at the job. It's about bringing out the best in others.** This is what separates those who are promoted because they were excellent at their previous role from those who are promoted because they will be excellent at developing people. This is what transforms a talented individual into a force multiplier. This is what creates organizations where people don't just do work—they grow, they contribute at their highest capacity, and they develop the maturity and skills to lead others. When you make this shift—when you stop measuring your leadership success by what you personally accomplish and start measuring it by what your team accomplishes, by how much they've grown, by the leaders they are becoming—everything changes. Your frustration with what you can't do yourself disappears because you've finally understood what you're actually supposed to be doing.

You're supposed to be developing people. Everything else flows from that.

Part – II

The Human Factor

04

The Power of Open-Mindedness

The Global Teams Reality

When organizations go global, they face a choice that will define everything that follows. They can approach it with genuine openness—recognizing that intelligence, innovation, and creativity are distributed across the world, not concentrated at headquarters. Or they can approach it with a closed mindset—assuming that the best thinking, the best decisions, and the best solutions all originate from the parent organization.

The difference between these two approaches is not subtle. It determines whether global partnerships thrive or simply survive. It determines whether you build a force multiplier or a source of friction. It determines whether you unlock the potential of talented people across the globe or waste it, I have seen both. And I can tell you: **open-mindedness is not optional for global teams. It is foundational.**

The Insecurity Trap

I would like to take the example of a Global Capability Center (GCC) where the formal relationship should be of a "Partner" between organizations headquarters and the offshore team. Though the higher management vision of working in a best cost country (BCC) is mainly cost, the bonus working is when the value & innovation starts to develop at par and slowly try to challenge and get past the parent organisation. Now, the challenge to the headquarters comes when the offshore team ambition grows to take more accountability and come out from the shadows of the headquarters and lead and be accountable towards the product directly. This is where the friction starts to grow at the operational levels of lower management at headquarters and the offshore teams. Till now there was a good amount of trust and a stable dependency with offshore teams adding value and efficiency to support the headquarters at their convenience and pace, but once the **ambition sets in**, the **insecurity grows.**

Here is what I have observed: global partnerships suffer most acutely when they operate from a place of insecurity and control. This is understandable, in a way. Organizations that expand globally face legitimate concerns. There are questions about job security—will offshore teams eventually take over the parent organization's roles? There are questions about influence—who makes the key decisions? There are questions about ownership—who drives the vision, who gets credit, who is ultimately accountable? These concerns are real. But how you handle them determines everything.

Some organizations respond by tightening control. They create approval gates for every decision. They keep knowledge siloed. They communicate selectively. They position the offshore team as the "delivery arm" rather than the "thinking arm." They send this message, sometimes overtly but more often subconsciously: *We will use you, but we won't trust you. We need your execution, but not your input.* Remember all this is happening at the operational levels where the power struggles remain to stay on a customer and vendor relationship, contradictory to the fact the higher management may be wanting to go a step further and make the accountability more open to the offshore teams as it suits the "cost" and "at par value" which can be sought from the offshore teams. What happens next is predictable. The offshore team senses the distrust. They recognize the control. And they begin to withdraw their discretionary effort, their innovation, their advocacy. The partnership doesn't fail outright—but it becomes transactional rather than collaborative. The organization then looks at the results and thinks: *See? We were right to be cautious.* But they miss the causal chain. They don't see that they created the very outcome they feared.

The Commitment Question

Here is the hard truth: **when an organization commits to a global path, it must do so with genuine intention and full effort.**

This means something specific. It means you are truly working to make the partnership succeed—not subconsciously (or overtly) proving that it cannot. It means you are genuinely open to the idea that your offshore partners might have better ideas than you do. It means you are willing to have your thinking challenged and changed. It means you are not waiting for failure so you can say, "I told you so."Because this dynamic exists more often than leaders care to admit. There are people in organizations who are sceptical about global collaboration. They doubt its viability. They worry about its implications. And whether consciously or unconsciously, they are invested in proving themselves right—in documenting why it doesn't work, why it can't work, why it shouldn't work.

What's more dangerous than failure is refusing to try.

If a global collaboration fails despite the best efforts of everyone involved—if you invested genuinely, communicated openly, took risks, supported your partners, and it still didn't work—then you have learned something valuable. You have gathered data. You have a foundation for the next iteration.

But if you start with a closed mindset, if you assume that all the best thinking resides only at headquarters, if you withhold trust and information, if you structure things so that failure is likely—then you're not conducting an experiment. You're engineering an outcome. And you're depriving yourself and your organization of the potential that existed all along.

The Survival Trap

There is another dangerous dynamic I have observed, and this one comes from the other direction.

Sometimes, teams on the other side of the world—often positioned as the delivery or support side—begin to give up. They sense the control. They feel the distrust. They recognize that their ideas are not welcomed, that their perspective is not valued, that pushing back will create friction. So, they make a choice: instead of advocating, instead of challenging, instead of bringing their full selves to the work, they fall into a pattern of mere survival.

They try to please their partners. They avoid conflict. They go quiet. They do what they are told. They stop asking difficult questions. They stop suggesting better ways. They stop taking risks.

This is a dangerous path. And I say this with conviction: **If we don't advocate for ourselves, if we don't challenge outdated thinking, if we don't bring our full capabilities to the table, we will perish—and not gracefully.**

The offshore team that accepts a subordinate role, that stops thinking critically, that prioritizes avoiding conflict over speaking truth—that team has already lost. They have given away their leverage. They have dimmed their light. They have chosen compliance over contribution.

And the parent organization has enabled it, even encouraged it.

This is not partnership. This is extraction.

The Foundation: Mutual Respect and Shared accountability

Real global partnerships are built on something entirely different.

They are built on **mutual respect**—genuine recognition that all parties bring value, expertise, and perspective to the table. Not hierarchical respect, where one side defers to the other. Mutual respect, where each side understands that the other side has something essential to contribute.

They are built on **shared accountability**—where success and failure belong to everyone, not where one side gets blamed for execution while the other side takes credit for thinking. When you share accountability, you share power. And when you share power, people stop playing politics and start playing to win.

They are built on **courage—on both sides.**

Courage from the headquarters side to genuinely listen, to challenge their own assumptions, to be open to the possibility that the better idea came from somewhere else. Courage to admit when they are wrong. Courage to give real authority, not the illusion of authority.

Courage from the offshore side to speak up even when it creates discomfort, to challenge decisions they believe are wrong, to advocate for their perspective, to refuse to accept a subordinate position in the partnership. Courage to say no when something doesn't make sense. Courage to lead, not just follow.

The Trust Equation

The best teams aren't built on control. They aren't built on approval gates and information silos and carefully managed authority.

They are built on trust.

And trust in a global context requires something specific: **it requires that you believe the people on the other side of the world are fundamentally capable, fundamentally motivated, and fundamentally invested in the same outcome as you are.**

When you operate from that belief—when you structure your collaboration around that belief—everything changes. You stop micromanaging because you trust judgment. You stop withholding information because you trust discretion. You stop making all the decisions because you trust the thinking. You stop assuming failure because you assume competence.

And the people on the other side? When they experience that trust, something shifts in them too. They stop protecting themselves. They stop playing it safe. They bring their full intelligence, their creativity, their innovation to the work. They become partners, not subordinates.

This is not naive optimism. This is not ignoring real challenges or pretending that global collaboration is easy. Global teams face genuine complexities: time zones, cultural differences, communication barriers, economic disparities, different working styles.

But these challenges can be managed. What cannot be managed is a fundamental lack of trust and openness.

The Choice Before You

Every leader building a global team faces a choice. It is perhaps the most consequential choice they will make about that partnership.

You can approach it with genuine open-mindedness—recognizing that your offshore partners are not a cost center or a delivery arm, but intellectual partners with capabilities and perspectives as valuable as your own. You can structure things around trust and mutual accountability. You can take risks. You can be vulnerable. You can let your thinking be challenged.

Or you can approach it with a closed mindset, a controlling stance, and an implicit message that you have already decided how this will turn out.

The first path requires courage. It requires releasing some control. It requires being genuinely open to being wrong.

But it is the only path that leads to real collaboration, real innovation, and real success on a global scale.

The choice is yours. But choose wisely—because your teams are watching, and they will respond in kind.

05

Supporting Effort, Not Just Results

The Question That Reveals Everything

Do you only reward results that are fruitful and punish or ignore failed efforts?

This question cuts to the heart of how you lead. Because the answer determines whether your team trusts you, whether they take risks, whether they bring their full selves to their work, and whether the culture you build is one where people grow or simply survive.

Most organizations operate on a results-only framework. They measure success by outcomes. They celebrate wins. They move on from losses—or worse, they publicly dissect them in ways that feel like punishment. The message, whether stated or implied, is clear: **Results are all that matter. Effort is irrelevant if it doesn't produce.**

This is where leadership breaks down.

The Problem with Results-Only Measurement

There are three fundamental problems with a results-only approach to performance.

- **First, binary thinking.** When you measure success only by results, you create a black-and-white worldview. You either win or you don't. You either delivered or you failed. You are either good enough or you're not. There is no middle ground. There is no nuance.

But real work—meaningful work, innovative work, work that matters—doesn't live in black and white. It lives in the shades of grey where effort meets uncertainty, where intention collides with complexity, where people are learning and growing and sometimes falling short even as they're genuinely trying.

Binary thinking is dangerous in environments where creativity matters, where learning matters, where experimentation matters. Because creativity requires risk. Learning requires failure. Experimentation requires outcomes you can't always predict. If the only acceptable outcome is success, you're not actually inviting people to create or learn or experiment. You're inviting them to play it safe.

- **Second, ignoring context.** Sometimes, the outcome has nothing to do with effort or capability. External factors impact results constantly: market shifts you couldn't have anticipated, budget limitations that weren't communicated clearly, timing that was beyond your control, luck—good and bad. A brilliant strategy executed perfectly can still fail because circumstances changed. A mediocre approach can succeed because of fortunate timing.

When you judge performance based only on results, ignoring context, you are making a fundamental attribution error. You are assuming that outcomes are always a direct result of individual effort and capability. You are ignoring the systems, the conditions, the luck, the timing that shape what actually happens.

This is unfair. More importantly, it is inaccurate. And people know it.

- **Third, it is demoralizing.** This is perhaps the most destructive consequence. When a person gives their best, brings their full effort, thinks carefully, takes smart risks, and the outcome still doesn't go as planned—and then that person is ignored, dismissed, or criticized—something breaks inside them.

The message they receive is: *Your effort wasn't good enough. Your best wasn't enough. Trying hard doesn't matter.*

Over time, this message kills motivation. It teaches people not to try. It teaches them to protect themselves, to minimize risk, to do the minimum required rather than going the extra mile. It teaches them that there is no point in bringing their full selves because even that won't be enough.

This is how organizations inadvertently create the mediocre, disengaged cultures they are trying to avoid.

True Leadership: Seeing Beyond the Scoreboard

Leadership requires something different. It requires a fundamental shift in how you measure and recognize contribution.

A leader sees beyond the scoreboard. They don't just look at the final result. They look at what happened along the way. They look at the choices people made. They look at the effort invested. They look at whether someone stretched themselves, whether they learned something, whether they grew in the process.

A leader knows when effort deserves recognition, even if the outcome didn't go as planned. They understand that recognizing effort is not the same as ignoring results. It is not lowering standards or pretending that failure is success. It is acknowledging that when someone has genuinely tried—when they have thought carefully, prepared well, executed with full commitment, and still come up short—that effort has value. That effort is worthy of recognition. That effort is what builds character and capability.

A leader stays with the overlooked, not just those celebrated. This is the test of real leadership. Anyone can show up for the winners. Anyone can celebrate success. The true measure of leadership is how you treat those who stumbled while trying. Do you disappear? Do you criticize? Or do you stay present, stay supportive, and help them learn and move forward?

This is where lasting cultures are built.

The Practical Path Forward

Supporting effort while maintaining accountability requires intentional practices. It requires a different way of communicating, recognizing, and developing people.

- **Celebrate Effort Publicly.** Don't wait for perfect results to recognize contribution. Acknowledge people for trying innovative things, even when those things don't work out. Recognize people for going the extra mile, for sticking to their values when it would have been easier to compromise, for persisting through difficulty. Do this publicly, not quietly. Let your team see that you value effort.

This serves multiple purposes. It signals what you actually value—not just outcomes, but integrity, courage, and commitment. It gives people permission to take risks, because they now know that intelligent failure won't be held against them. And it builds a culture where people want to bring their full effort, because they know it will be seen and appreciated.

- **Give Constructive Feedback.** When effort falls short of results, resist the urge to just move on or assign blame. Instead, create space for reflection and learning. Help the person understand what happened. What did they learn? What would they do differently next time? What support do they need to be more effective?

This is not about making them feel better. It is about helping them grow. Constructive feedback says: *I believe in your capability. I believe you can learn from this. I'm invested in your development, not just your current performance.*

- **Protect Psychological Safety.** Create an environment where it is explicitly safe to fail, as long as the effort was genuine. This means establishing clear boundaries—what kinds of failures are acceptable? What does "genuine effort" actually look like? What will not be tolerated? Then, within those boundaries, make it clear that intelligent risk-taking and occasional failure are expected, not punished.

Psychological safety doesn't mean there are no consequences. It means that consequences are proportional and fair. It means that failures are treated as learning opportunities, not character flaws. It means that people are not publicly shamed or made to feel small for trying and falling short.

- **Balance Recognition Across the Spectrum.** Applaud success, absolutely. Celebrate wins. Recognize achievements. But don't only show up for photo ops when things go right. Be just as visible, just as present, and just as appreciative when people are in the struggle. Show up for the person who gave their best and fell short. Show up for the person who is learning and making mistakes. Show up for the person who is still trying after multiple failures.

This presence—this visibility and support across all circumstances—is what builds trust. People know you're not just a fair-weather leader. They know you're committed to them, not just their performance.

- **Balancing Accountability and Empathy.** Here is the question many leaders ask: "If I recognize effort even when results fall short, won't I be lowering accountability?" No. You are redefining it.

Accountability is not about punishment. It is about responsibility. It is about each person owning their choices, their effort, their learning, and their growth. You can hold someone fully accountable for bringing their best effort while also being empathetic about the outcome.

In fact, these two things are inseparable. Real accountability only works when it is paired with empathy. Because if people feel judged, if they feel unsafe, if they fear that a misstep will result in punishment or public humiliation, they will not be honest about their challenges. They will not ask for help. They will not take risks. They will not learn.

But if they feel supported—if they know that you care about their growth, that you will stand by them when they struggle, that you see their effort and appreciate it—then they will own their mistakes. They will ask for help. They will reflect honestly. They will commit to change.

This is true accountability.

The True Measure of Leadership

A leader's true measure is not how they treat the winners. Everyone can applaud success. Everyone can celebrate those who delivered.

The true measure of leadership is how you stand by those who stumble while trying.

It is whether you remain human, empathetic, and value-driven—especially in failure. It is whether you recognize that people are not reducible to their quarterly results, that human beings have depth and complexity and seasons, that sometimes the greatest growth happens in moments of struggle.

When you lead this way—when you support effort alongside results, when you balance accountability with empathy, when you show up for people in all seasons—you build a culture where people don't just perform. They grow. They contribute. They bring their full selves. And paradoxically, this is where the best results eventually come from.

Not from fear or pressure, but from people who know they are valued, who feel safe to try, who understand that their effort matters regardless of the immediate outcome.

This is where lasting cultures are built.

06

The Trap of Control and the Art of Letting Go

The Daily Struggle

Every day is a desperate attempt to survive, prove yourself again, and simply be visible.

If you recognize this feeling, you are not alone. And if this sentence resonates with something deep inside you, it's time to ask yourself a harder question: Is this leadership, or is this survival?

There is a difference.

Leaders who operate from this place—constantly pushing, constantly proving, constantly ensuring they remain visible and valued—are not leading. They are performing. They are trapped in a loop that looks like leadership from the outside but feels like drowning from the inside.

The strange thing about this trap is that it is often mistaken for excellence. We celebrate people who work this hard. We admire their dedication. We assume that their constant effort is what makes them effective. But effectiveness and exhaustion are not the same thing. And leadership that requires someone to be at 110% every single day is not sustainable—not for the leader, and certainly not for the team that has to keep up with that pace.

Control: The Illusion We Believe In

At the root of this daily struggle is something more fundamental: **the belief that you can control outcomes.**

You already know this isn't true. Rationally, you understand that not everything is within your control. Market conditions shift. People make unexpected choices. External factors intervene. Timing is off. Luck plays a role. You cannot control it all, no matter how hard you try.

And yet, the urge to control outcomes remains so deeply embedded that letting go feels terrifying.

Because here is what haunts you: What happens if you stop pushing? Will people forget you? Will things fall apart? Will you disappear?

These questions feel existential. And that's the clue that something deeper is at play.

You Are Not Broken—You Are Conditioned

The urge to control isn't a moral failing. It's not a character flaw that needs to be overcome through sheer willpower. It is a **survival mechanism.**

Somewhere along the line—perhaps early in your career, perhaps in your family, perhaps in a moment of profound vulnerability—you learned that being in control, or being exceptional, was the only way to feel safe or valued. You learned that if you didn't push, if you didn't prove yourself, if you didn't stay visible, you would get overlooked. Or hurt. Or dismissed.

So, you adapted. You developed the ability to push harder than others, to think faster, to prepare more thoroughly, to stay visible and relevant. This adaptation served you. It protected you. It got you to where you are.

But protections that once served us can become prisons.

The defence mechanism that kept you safe is now keeping you trapped. And the exhausting part is this: it works just well enough that you can't quite let it go. Because every time you stay visible, every time you prove yourself, you get validation. You get recognition. You get evidence that your exhausting approach is necessary, is working, is justified.

So, you keep doing it. And you keep being exhausted.

But here's what you need to understand: **You are not broken. You are conditioned.** And conditioning can be unconditioned.

Letting Go Doesn't Mean Giving Up

One of the greatest myths about leadership is that effectiveness requires constant, maximum effort. That letting up means you care less. That stepping back means you've given up.

This is not true.

Letting things play out naturally is not laziness. It is not failure. It is not a sign of weakness or declining commitment. It is a **different understanding of what your job actually is.**

Your job is not to control outcomes. Your job is not to be visible in every decision, every conversation, every initiative. Your job is not to ensure that people know you were involved, that you got credit, that you maintained influence.

Your actual job—your real job—is the effort you bring. The intention you carry. The values you model. The systems you put in place. The people you develop. The direction you set. And then, crucially, **the trust you extend to others to execute.**

Everything else is noise.

When you can distinguish between what is actually your responsibility and what is not, something shifts. You stop needing to be in every room. You stop needing to have the final say. You stop needing to prove that your involvement made the difference. Because you understand: **your value isn't measured by how much you control—it's measured by what you enable.**

A leader who enables others to succeed, who creates conditions where teams can thrive without constant oversight, who develops people so capable that the team functions well even when the leader steps back—that is a leader with true leverage. That is a multiplier.

The irony is this: leaders who learn to let go often become more effective, not less. Because the energy they were spending on control becomes available for strategy, vision, and development. Because teams that are trusted become more capable. Because the outcomes that emerge from genuine autonomy often exceed what micromanagement ever produced.

The Hard Truth About Rest

Here is something that runs counter to everything you've been taught: **You deserve rest without needing to earn it.**

The idea that you can only rest after proving your worth each day is a trap. It's a trap because the proving never actually stops. There's always another goal. Always another way to be seen. Always another opportunity to demonstrate your value.

You don't have to be at 110% every single day just to deserve space or calm. You don't have to be exceptional, productive, or visible to deserve a break. You are allowed to exist without performing. Even if no one notices. Even if nothing gets done.

This sounds radical because we live in a culture that equates rest with laziness and productivity with worth. But consider what this belief costs you: exhaustion. Burnout. The constant anxiety that you're not doing enough. The inability to simply be, without the pressure to prove.

The rest you deserve isn't something you need to earn through superior performance. It is your birthright as a human being. And the sooner you claim it, the sooner you can actually be present—to your work, to your team, to your own life—in a way that isn't driven by fear.

Visibility Isn't the Same as Value

In today's world, visibility is a powerful currency. Being seen, being heard, being in the center of things carries real weight. Organizations often reward visibility. Careers are built on it. Power flows to those who are most visible.

So, it makes sense that you've chased it. It makes sense that staying visible feels essential.

But here is the fundamental truth: **Your value is not determined by how visible you are.**

Your value is not based on how loud you are in meetings. It is not based on how many decisions you influence. It is not based on how much credit you receive. It is not based on how many people notice what you contribute.

Your value is based on who you are and what you enable. It is based on the integrity you bring. The growth you facilitate in others. The direction you set. The culture you shape. The trust you build.

And here's what happens when you measure yourself by visibility alone: you will always feel like you're fading. Because visibility is fleeting. Being in the spotlight today doesn't guarantee it tomorrow. Someone else will eventually be louder, or more visible, or more talked about. And if your entire sense of value is tied to being seen, then you are always in a precarious position.

But if your value is rooted in something deeper—in the work you do, the people you develop, the values you embody—then visibility becomes irrelevant. You don't need to chase it. You don't need to prove it. You simply are.

This is freedom.

The Practice: Loosening the Grip

Letting go completely, all at once, is terrifying. And it's not practical. If you've spent years in control mode, suddenly attempting full surrender will likely feel impossible—and you'll probably bounce right back into old patterns.

Instead, try loosening your grip in tiny, safe ways. Test letting go in small areas where the stakes feel manageable. Where if things don't go perfectly, it won't shake your foundations.

- **Skip a task you'd normally over-prepare for.** Leave some things undone or less polished than you'd prefer. Notice that the world doesn't end. Notice that people don't judge you as harshly as you fear.

- **Let someone else take the lead, even if it's imperfect.** Resist the urge to correct them, to step in, to make sure it's done your way. Give them room to find their own approach. Often, it won't be how you would have done it—and often, it will still be good. Sometimes, it will even be better.
- **Choose silence instead of explanation.** When your instinct is to justify your decision, to explain your thinking, to ensure people understand your rationale, try staying quiet instead. Let the decision speak for itself. Let people form their own conclusions. See what happens.

Often, nothing bad happens. Often, there is peace.

And in that peace, you might discover something important: the outcomes you were so afraid of losing by letting go? They unfold anyway. The people you were afraid would forget you without constant visibility? They remember. The value you were afraid would disappear without constant proving? It persists.

This is when the real shift begins. When you have evidence—not just intellectual understanding, but actual lived experience—that control was the problem, not the solution.

The Path Forward

This is not about becoming passive. It is not about checking out or caring less. It is about understanding that **your worth is not negotiable.** It doesn't need to be earned daily. It doesn't require constant proof.

- You can lead without controlling. You can be valuable without being visible. You can create extraordinary outcomes without being at 110% every single day.

And in letting go of the need to control, you don't lose power. You actually find it—the kind of power that comes from trust, from delegation, from enabling others to be at their best. The kind of power that doesn't require constant effort to maintain.

- Loosen the grip. Test it in small ways. And notice what emerges when you finally allow things to play out naturally. Because you might just discover that the outcomes you were so afraid of losing were never yours to control in the first place.

They were always meant to unfold on their own.

And your job—your real job—is simply to create the conditions where they could.

07

Fairness vs. Equality in Leadership

The Fundamental Confusion

There is a confusion that runs through many organizations, whispered in hallways and voiced in complaints: "Why did they get that and I didn't? We do the same job. This is unfair."

And leaders, wanting to be good people, want to fix it. They want to ensure that everyone gets treated the same way. They want to distribute opportunities equally. They want everyone to feel valued and included.

But here is where good intentions collide with reality: **Fairness and equality are not the same thing.**

And confusing them is one of the most damaging mistakes a leader can make.

In a world of limited resources—and every organization operates with limits—not everyone can receive the same outcomes at the same time. There are only so many promotions. Only so many project leadership opportunities. Only so much recognition budget. Only so much compensation to distribute. The math is simple: there are more people than there are rewards.

So, the question becomes: How do you distribute these limited resources in a way that feels fair, even when everyone cannot have the same outcome?

The answer lies in understanding that fairness is not about giving everyone the same thing. Fairness is about how you make decisions about who gets what.

What True Fairness Actually Looks Like

True fairness in the workplace is built on four foundational principles.

- **First, providing equal access to opportunities.** This means that the door is open to everyone. There are no hidden pathways that favour the chosen few. Everyone knows how to be considered for a promotion, how to be selected for a high-visibility project, how to earn recognition. The criteria are transparent. The process is accessible. Your background, your network, your relationship with the boss doesn't determine whether you even get a chance.

Equal access doesn't guarantee equal outcomes. But it ensures that outcomes are based on merit, not privilege.

- **Second, setting clear expectations.** People cannot meet a standard they don't understand. If you want to be fair, you must be explicit about what success looks like. What does a high performer actually do? What behaviour's, contributions, and results do you recognize? What are the gaps between someone who is performing at an acceptable level and someone who is performing at an exceptional level?

When expectations are clear, people can calibrate their effort accordingly. They can understand exactly what it takes to be in the running for the opportunity they want. And when they are not selected, they can understand why—not because of favouritism, but because they didn't meet the explicit standard.

- **Third, recognizing performance and merit.** Fairness means that you are actually paying attention to what people accomplish. You are tracking contributions. You are observing effort and impact. And you are connecting those observations to your decisions. The person who went the extra mile gets recognized. The person who delivered exceptional results gets considered for advancement. The person who grew significantly gets acknowledged.

Merit-based recognition is the opposite of favouritism. It is visible, defensible, and reproducible. Anyone who puts in similar effort and achieves similar results can expect similar recognition.

- **Fourth, being transparent in how decisions are made.** This is perhaps the most critical element. People can accept outcomes they don't like if they understand how those outcomes were determined. They can accept that they weren't selected if they understand the process, the criteria, and how they fell short. But when decisions feel opaque, when the reasoning is unclear, when people don't understand why someone else was chosen, then fairness becomes invisible—and the decision feels like favouritism regardless of how fair it actually was.

Transparency is the bridge between fairness and perception.

The Honest Part: Not Everyone Will Be Happy

Here is the truth that many leaders struggle to accept: **even when you are fair and transparent, some team members may feel overlooked or disappointed.**

This is not a failure of fairness. This is not a sign that your system is broken. This is simply part of leadership.

Because fairness is not about pleasing everyone. It is not about ensuring that every person feels equally valued or equally advanced or equally recognized. Fairness is about making principled decisions that you can explain and defend, even if not everyone likes the outcome.

This distinction matters. Because if you measure the success of your fairness system by whether everyone is happy, you will fail. You will end up either distributing everything equally in an attempt to keep everyone satisfied, or you will abandon your principles in the face of complaint.

Neither of these is fair.

Real fairness sometimes means disappointing people. It means telling someone they didn't get the promotion, but here's why and here's what they need to do next time. It means saying no to a request, but explaining the reasoning behind that no. It means recognizing one person's achievement over another's, even though both people worked hard.

The goal is not to minimize dissatisfaction. The goal is to **minimize favouritism.** To ensure that decisions are based on principles, not personalities. To ensure that outcomes reflect merit, not relationships. To ensure that if someone asks why a particular decision was made, you can answer with clarity and conviction.

How to Build Credibility Through Fairness

There are concrete practices that separate leaders who are genuinely fair from those who just say they are.

- **Communicate decisions openly.** Don't make a decision and then disappear. Don't announce outcomes without explanation. Take the time to explain the "why" behind your choices. Why was this person selected for the role? Why didn't that person get the promotion? Why is this investment being made in this direction?

When you communicate openly, you serve multiple purposes. You signal that you have nothing to hide. You give people the information they need to understand and, ideally, accept the decision. And you create a foundation of trust—people see that you are willing to be transparent, and they are more likely to trust your motives.

- **Give feedback to those not chosen.** This is where many leaders fail. They make a decision about who gets an opportunity, announce it, and then never talk to the people who didn't get it. Those people are left to assume, to wonder, to feel rejected.

Instead, take time to meet with each person who wasn't selected. Help them understand the gap between where they are and where they need to be to be competitive next time. Be specific. Be honest. Help them see a path forward.

This accomplishes something crucial: it transforms a moment of rejection into a moment of investment. The person who didn't get selected experiences your leadership not as dismissal, but as mentorship. They understand what they need to work on. They see that you care enough to help them improve. And they are more likely to stay motivated and engaged, rather than becoming resentful or checked out.

- **Offer paths for growth.** Make it clear that not getting an opportunity today doesn't mean you don't believe in someone's potential. Help them see what development would make them competitive. What skills do they need to develop? What experiences would help them? What feedback should they act on?

When people feel like they're being developed, even when they don't get what they wanted immediately, they remain motivated. They see the fairness as genuine—not a system that is rigged against them, but a system that is challenging them to grow.

- **Be consistent over time.** This is the multiplier effect of fairness. People may not agree with every single decision you make. They may feel disappointed by an outcome that goes against them. But over time, if you consistently apply the same principles, if you consistently explain your reasoning, if you consistently recognize merit and minimize favouritism, people will develop confidence in your fairness.

They will see that you treat others with the same transparency and principle-based decision-making that you extend to them. They will see that you are not arbitrarily favouring anyone. They will respect your integrity, even when they don't like a particular outcome.

This consistency is what builds credibility. It says: "You can trust this leader. Even if I disagree with a decision, I know it was made fairly."

The Practice of Principled Decision-Making

Fairness is not arbitrary. It is not based on mood or preference. It is based on principles that you establish, communicate, and then apply consistently.

Before you make a significant decision—who gets the promotion, who leads the project, whose work gets highlighted—ask yourself these questions:

- **What principle is driving this decision?** Are you selecting based on merit and demonstrated performance? Are you allocating based on opportunity and development? Are you recognizing based on contribution? Be clear about your principle. Write it down if you need to.
- **Can I explain this principle to others?** If you cannot articulate why this principle matters, or if you struggle to explain it to your team, then you probably haven't clarified it enough. Go deeper. Refine it until you can speak about it with clarity and conviction.
- **Does my decision actually reflect this principle?** Once you've established your principle, check your decision against it. Are you being consistent? Are you actually following what you said you would follow? Or are you letting other factors—favouritism, convenience, politics—subtly influence the outcome?
- **Can I defend this decision to anyone who questions it?** This is the final test. If you made this decision and had to explain it to the person who disagreed with it, to your boss, to your entire team, could you do so with confidence? Could you show them the principle and show them how your decision reflects that principle?

If you cannot confidently answer yes to this question, go back and reconsider. Either your principle is not clear, or your decision does not reflect it.

The Credibility Equation

Here is what happens when you lead with fairness: people develop faith in your judgment. Not because they always agree with you, but because they trust that you are thinking clearly and acting with integrity.

They know that if they work hard and contribute meaningfully, they will be recognized—not guaranteed to get the specific outcome they want, but recognized. They know that if they want an opportunity, the criteria are clear and the door is open. They know that if they don't get selected, you will explain why and help them understand what to do next.

This faith transforms your team. People stop playing politics. They stop worrying about whether they're favoured. They stop spending energy trying to understand the hidden rules. Instead, they invest their energy in doing excellent work, in growing, in contributing.

And your credibility—your ability to influence, to be believed, to lead effectively—grows as a result. Because credibility is not built on being liked. It is built on being fair, being transparent, and being consistent.

The Final Principle

Remember this: **fairness is not about giving everyone the same thing. Fairness is about giving everyone a fair shot and then making principled decisions about how to allocate limited resources.**

When you lead with this understanding, when you build systems and practices that reflect this principle, when you communicate openly and apply consistency, you create a culture where people may not always get what they want, but they trust that they've been treated fairly.

And that trust—that credibility—is worth more than unanimous happiness. Because it allows you to lead with integrity. It allows your team to perform at their best. And it allows you to make the difficult decisions that good leadership sometimes requires, with the confidence that your people will respect your judgment, even if they don't always like the outcome.

This is fairness. And this is how credibility is built.

08

Empathetic Leadership

The Technical Leader's Journey

Coming from a technical background, I was wired a certain way. Focus on delivery. Measure by performance. Track outcomes. Close the loop. Move on.

In the fast-moving world of engineering and operations, this approach made sense. It felt efficient. It felt rational. Relationships were transactional—you had a task, you completed it, and you both moved forward. Emotions were secondary to execution. Feelings were less important than results.

This is how I thought leadership worked.

But over years of leading teams, watching people succeed and fail, observing what actually built loyalty versus what just produced compliance, I came to realize something that my technical mind resisted: **being an empathetic leader is not just more rewarding—it's more effective.**

And this realization changed everything about how I lead.

What Empathetic Leadership Actually Is

Here is what empathetic leadership is not: it is not being soft. It is not lowering expectations. It is not avoiding difficult conversations or sidestepping accountability. It is not pretending that performance doesn't matter or that results are optional.

Here is what it actually is: **pausing to understand the person behind the role.**

It is asking: What are they going through right now? How are they feeling about their work, their role, their trajectory? What pressures are they facing that I might not see? What strengths do they have that might be going unrecognized? What is getting in the way of them performing at their best?

Empathetic leadership means recognizing that the human side and the performance side are not separate. They are intimately connected. How someone feels, what they're struggling with, whether they feel seen and valued—all of this impacts their performance. It impacts their energy. It impacts their willingness to go the extra mile. It impacts whether they stay or leave.

The technical leader in me thought these were distractions from the real work. But I was wrong. Understanding the human side is not a distraction. It is foundational. Because you cannot actually unlock someone's full potential without understanding what might be blocking it.

The Shift That Changes Everything

I've seen firsthand what happens when you take the time to connect emotionally—even briefly—with someone who is struggling. When you ask genuinely difficult questions. When you listen to their side of the story without immediately jumping to judgment. When you work through challenges alongside them rather than standing apart from them.

Something shifts.

There's renewed energy. There's trust where there was previously wariness. There's often a deeper sense of loyalty and ownership from that person, and it radiates to the rest of the team. Because when people see a leader choose empathy in a moment where they could have chosen judgment, they learn something about your values. They learn that you see them as more than just their output. They learn that you're willing to pause and understand before you act.

This is not soft leadership. This is actually the most practical leadership there is. Because the alternative—transactional, detached leadership—produces compliance at best and resentment at worst. It keeps people in a state of anxiety, not inspiration. It discourages risk-taking and honesty. It teaches people to hide their struggles rather than bring them forward.

But empathetic leadership produces something different: it produces people who want to contribute, not just because they have to, but because they feel valued and understood.

The Moment That Mattered

I remember a particularly unusual situation that taught me more about leadership than any textbook could have.

One of my team members was struggling to integrate at the client's end. The integration was important. It was expected to go smoothly. But it wasn't. There were friction points. There were misalignments. There were concerns about capability and fit.

The pressure from higher management was clear and unambiguous: "Let him go."

On the surface, this made sense. The situation wasn't working. The client was unhappy. The path of least resistance was to replace him with someone else. A transactional leader—the person I used to be—would have made that decision quickly. Remove the problem. Find a replacement. Move on.

But something didn't sit right with me.

So instead of rushing to a decision, I took the time to understand his side of the story. I had an open conversation with him. I asked questions I might have otherwise skipped: What was he experiencing? What was he observing? Where did he feel unsupported? Where were the actual gaps, and where was he being unfairly judged?

What I uncovered wasn't a failure on his part. It was a mismatch of expectations and context. The client had certain assumptions about how he should operate that were never explicitly communicated. His working style, which was perfectly effective in our environment, didn't align with their culture and processes. He wasn't being given the information he needed to succeed. And he was bearing the brunt of blame for a situation that was actually systemic.

Once I understood this, I didn't just accept the situation—I acted on it. I had open conversations with both him and the client. We reframed the situation. We aligned on expectations. We created a bridge between his strengths and what the client actually needed. We arrived at a much fairer resolution.

That employee went on to perform significantly better. Not because he suddenly became more capable—he was capable all along. But because the right environment and support were put in place. Because he experienced leadership that chose to understand before choosing to dismiss.

The Alternative Path

I think about what would have happened if I had taken the other route.

If I had accepted the pressure to let him go, if I had prioritized short-term ease over understanding, if I had treated him as a problem to be removed rather than a person to be understood—what would have happened?

He would have lost his position. He would have been sent a message that when things get difficult, when alignment isn't immediate, he's expendable. He would have left the organization carrying hurt, resentment, and a story about a leader who didn't believe in him.

The team would have observed all of this. They would have learned: when a leader doesn't understand you, you're at risk. When things get difficult, management will abandon you rather than work through it with you. The message is: be careful. Protect yourself. Don't trust that your leader will actually invest in understanding you.

And I would have lost a capable person and damaged my credibility with the rest of the team, all in the name of short-term efficiency.

But that's not what happened. Because I chose differently.

The Cost of Not Choosing Empathy

This story is not unique. I have seen versions of it play out across organizations. A person struggles. Management sees it as a performance problem. The instinct is to remove the problem. The person is let go, transferred, or pushed out.

Sometimes, there are legitimate reasons for that outcome. Not every situation can be salvaged. Not every mismatch can be fixed. But often—far more often than we admit—the person on the other side of that decision was capable, was trying, was just missing the understanding, support, or context they needed.

When you don't take the time to understand, you don't just lose that person. You lose the potential they represented. You lose the loyalty of the people watching. You damage your credibility as someone who will work with people through difficulty versus someone who will discard them when things get complex.

And you reinforce a culture where people learn to hide, to protect themselves, to not bring their authentic struggles to their leaders. Because they've seen what happens when you do—you become a problem to be solved, not a person to be understood.

What Empathetic Leadership Actually Requires

Empathetic leadership is not passive. It requires active choices and clear boundaries.

- **It requires the willingness to pause.** When something isn't working, the instinct is often to act quickly. But empathy requires pausing. Taking time. Asking questions. Listening to understand, not to confirm your initial judgment.
- **It requires genuine curiosity.** You have to actually want to understand the other person's experience. You have to be open to the possibility that your initial perception might be incomplete or

wrong. You have to ask questions and really listen to the answers.

- **It requires accountability.** Understanding someone's struggle doesn't mean ignoring performance gaps. It means addressing them together. It means being clear about expectations and being willing to work through challenges—but also being clear about what needs to shift for this to work.
- **It requires boundaries.** Empathy is not acceptance of everything. You can understand someone's struggle and still require growth. You can see their humanity and still hold them accountable. Empathy with boundaries is how you actually develop people.
- **It requires seeing the whole person.** The person in front of you is not just their role. They are someone with dreams, fears, pressures, and capabilities that extend far beyond what you see in their job. When you see that whole person, when you recognize their humanity, everything shifts.

The Earlier We Start, The Better

As leaders, we don't always get taught this early. Many of us come from technical or functional backgrounds where the focus was on what people produce, not who they are. We learned to measure success by outcomes, not by the human impact of how we achieve those outcomes.

But here is what I've learned: **the earlier we embrace empathetic leadership, the more resilient, motivated, and connected our teams become.**

Teams that experience empathetic leadership take more risks because they know a thoughtful leader will work with them through failure. They communicate more openly because they've experienced being understood. They stay longer because they feel valued as whole people, not just their output. They perform better because they're motivated by connection, not just compliance.

This is not soft. This is strategic. This is how you actually build organizations where people do their best work.

Leading With Clarity and Heart

The technical leader in me hasn't gone anywhere. I still believe in clarity. I still value outcomes. I still track performance and hold people accountable.

But I've learned to do all of that while also seeing the person. While also pausing to understand. While also choosing empathy when I could choose judgment.

This is not a trade-off. This is actually the integration that makes leadership work.

Let's lead with clarity, but also with heart. Let's set clear expectations and also take time to understand what's getting in the way of people meeting them. Let's measure performance and also recognize the human effort behind that performance. Let's hold people accountable and also stand by them when they struggle.

This is empathetic leadership. And it is far more powerful than the transactional approach I started with. Because people don't just work harder for leaders they respect. They work differently, they think differently, they commit differently—when they know they're genuinely understood.

That is the shift. That is the difference. And that is why empathy is not just more rewarding—it's more effective.

Part – III

Leading in the Modern World

09

The Paradox of AI for Mechanical Engineers

The Real Question: Visibility vs. Impact

The actual risk isn't that mechanical engineering will become irrelevant—it will become *invisible.*

We'll still need great mechanical engineers, probably more than ever. But if we don't intentionally value and celebrate that work, talented people will chase visibility instead of impact.

That's not a technological problem. It's a leadership and culture problem. And those are solvable.

The Invisibility Crisis

AI and software now dominate boardroom conversations, media coverage, and career narratives. Mechanical engineering risks becoming the "unsexy infrastructure layer"—absolutely essential, taken for granted, but starved of attention and prestige.

A software engineer training a neural network for autonomous driving gets visibility, conference talks, and the narrative. A mechanical engineer solving a critical thermal management challenge for EV battery housings works on something equally complex, equally important to vehicle safety and performance—but nobody's writing about it. Nobody's featuring them on LinkedIn.

Talented young engineers choosing their specializations see this clearly. Visibility matters. If the field they choose is invisible, even if it's impactful, they feel that weight over a 40-year career. Eventually, many choose differently.

The Talent Pipeline Risk

Today's generation of mechanical engineers will continue to be in demand. But watch the next generation—the high school students, undergraduate engineers, early-career professionals deciding where to focus their energy. They're absorbing the cultural signals about what matters.

If mechanical engineering is consistently portrayed as "keeping the lights on" rather than "building the future," attrition follows. Not because the work isn't needed, but because humans want their contributions recognized and celebrated.

Why This Is Actually Solvable

The encouraging part: **this isn't a technology problem—it's a choice.**

Adding more AI tools to mechanical engineering doesn't solve invisibility. The solution requires deliberate cultural and leadership decisions that are completely within your control.

- ➢ **Counter the Visibility Bias.** Make mechanical engineering work visible and celebrated internally and externally. Don't assume good work speaks for itself—it doesn't.

When a structural breakthrough saves 2kg *and* improves crash safety, celebrate it. When a materials innovation solves a thermal cycling problem, highlight it with the same prominence as a new autonomous driving stack update.

- ➢ **Reflect That All Layers Matter Equally.** Vehicle safety, performance, and innovation depend on every discipline. Not just the headline-grabbing AI features.

Mechanical engineering in the AI era isn't about defending the past—it's about recognizing that every AI-powered innovation still lives inside a *physical system* that must perform reliably, safely, and efficiently. That's not legacy work. That's the foundation.

- **Build Integrated Teams, Not Silos.** The best work happens when mechanical, software, and systems engineers collaborate as equals from day one—not when one layer implements the other's requirements.

Structure cross-functional teams so no discipline dominates the narrative, even unintentionally.

- **Reward Impact, Not Just Visibility.** Ensure talented mechanical engineers see a clear path to leadership and influence. Show them their career can be as rewarding as any other engineering path.
- **Partner on Education.** Work with universities and technical programs to emphasize the intellectual richness of mechanical engineering in an AI-driven world. Stop positioning it as legacy work.

The Deeper Question

The observation reveals a choice being made—often unconsciously—about what kinds of engineering problems we celebrate and what kinds we take for granted.

That choice will shape which engineers we attract, how we develop them, and ultimately, what innovations we're capable of creating.

The question isn't whether mechanical engineering will survive AI. It will. The question is whether it will thrive—and whether the next generation will want to be part of it.

That answer depends entirely on leadership and culture. It's not predetermined. It's solvable.

And it starts with making the invisible visible.

The Path Forward

This isn't about nostalgia. It's about clarity.

The organizations that will thrive in the next decade will be the ones that intentionally value and celebrate the full spectrum of engineering excellence. From the algorithms processing sensor data to the materials withstanding thermal cycling. From the autonomous driving stacks to the crash structures that save lives.

Every layer matters. Leadership must make that visible—in how teams are structured, how work is celebrated, and where career paths lead.

The power to do this is entirely in your hands.

10

Accountability in the Hybrid Era

The Real Dilemma

We're asking the wrong question.

Instead of "Is someone working from home truly productive?" we should be asking: "Are we measuring what actually matters?"

The hybrid work era exposed a fundamental flaw in how organizations think about accountability. For decades, we conflated presence with productivity, cameras on with commitment, hours logged with output delivered. Hybrid work didn't create new problems—it made visible the problems that were always there.

Now we face a choice: evolve how we define and measure accountability, or double down on surveillance and control. Many organizations are choosing the latter. That's a mistake.

The Three Impossible Questions

When someone works from home, leadership often finds itself tangled in three contradictory anxieties:

Are they truly productive? We can't see them working, so we assume they might not be.

Are they overworking silently without boundaries? We can't see them stopping, so we assume they might burn out.

Are they simply overwhelmed by the lack of structure? We can't see them struggling, so we assume they might drown.

All three could be true. None of them are visible through a camera. All three are answered not by surveillance, but by clarity: outcome alignment, regular check-ins, clear expectations, and genuine feedback loops.

Yet many organizations' response has been to install monitoring software, mandate camera presence, or implement keystroke tracking. This approach rests on a dangerous assumption: **that you can force accountability through visibility.**

You can't. What you force through visibility is compliance. And compliance looks nothing like accountability.

The Policy Problem Nobody's Talking About

There's something else happening beneath the surface of hybrid work struggles—something that makes building trust even harder.

Labour codes and policies are shifting in ways that undermine the very foundation hybrid work needs: predictability and protection for the workforce.

When the threshold for mandatory government approval before layoffs rise from 100 to 300 employees, what message does that send to workers? That job security just became more fragile. When 12-hour workdays become permissible "in the name of flexibility," often without fair overtime compensation, who wins that trade?

Hybrid work already creates uncertainty. Employees don't know if they're being evaluated fairly. They don't know if their remote work will be held against them in promotion decisions. They don't know if the flexibility they've been granted is real or temporary.

Add policy-level insecurity on top of that—weaker labour protections, higher layoff thresholds, longer workdays without corresponding compensation—and you've created an environment where trust cannot exist. You've structured it to fail.

Employees sense this. They feel less protected. Managers, in turn, feel pressure to do more monitoring, implement more controls, demand more visibility. Not because they want to, but because the system is signalling that flexibility is a liability that needs to be managed.

It's a spiral. And it starts not with bad management, but with bad policy.

What Accountability Actually Requires

Accountability in the hybrid era is fundamentally different from accountability in a physical office. It has to be.

You can't see it. So, you have to be clear about it.

1. Redefine Productivity by Outcomes, Not Presence

Stop measuring hours. Stop measuring time online. Stop measuring camera status.

Measure what was delivered. Measure what was completed. Measure what moved forward. Measure quality. Measure collaboration. Measure impact.

This requires managers to do harder work—they have to know what "done" looks like, they have to communicate it clearly, and they have to track it consistently. But that's not a bug. That's a feature.

When you're forced to articulate what success looks like, you tend to get clearer about what actually matters. And that clarity is the foundation of accountability—hybrid or not.

For engineering teams, this means: Does the design work? Does it meet the requirements? Did it integrate cleanly with other systems? Was it delivered on schedule? These are measurable. These are objective. These don't require anyone to be visible.

2. Push for Labour Reforms that Protect Today's Workforce

This is where the conversation gets uncomfortable for many leaders, but it's unavoidable.

Accountability can't be one-directional. If you ask employees to be accountable for their performance, their focus, their outcomes—you cannot simultaneously strip away the protections that allow them to take that accountability seriously.

Hybrid workers need:

- Clear policies on work hours and boundaries
- Transparent criteria for performance evaluation
- Protection from arbitrary layoffs based on remote status
- Fair compensation for all time worked
- Job security that matches their organizational contribution

These aren't nice-to-haves. They're the prerequisites for two-way accountability. Without them, employees optimize for self-protection, not performance. They work longer hours to prove they're not slacking. They stay visible to avoid being cut. They hoard information to protect their position.

That's not accountability. That's fear.

Labour reform matters. Advocating for it matters. And if your organization operates in jurisdictions where labour protections are eroding, you have a responsibility to engage in that conversation—not as a capitalist vs. labour issue, but as a business sustainability issue.

The organizations that attract and retain top talent in the hybrid era will be the ones that offer genuine protection alongside genuine flexibility.

3. Lead with Empathy, Not Surveillance

Surveillance is the lazy answer to accountability.

It *feels* like control. It *feels* like you're managing risk. But what it actually does is damage the exact thing you need most in hybrid work: trust.

When you implement keystroke monitoring, it tells employees: "We assume you're not working unless we can prove it."

When you mandate camera presence, it tells employees: "Your face is more important than your focus."

When you require location tracking, it tells employees: "We don't trust you."

And then you're surprised when they don't feel accountable to you.

Empathy-led accountability works differently. It starts with recognizing that people are trying to do their jobs under uncertain conditions. Some are thriving in hybrid work. Some are struggling. Some are burning out silently. Most are navigating a mix of all three at different times.

Regular check-ins matter. Not status updates—real conversations. "How are you actually doing?" "Are the boundaries working for you?" "What's blocking you right now?" "What do you need from me?"

This is harder than surveillance. It requires attention. It requires presence—even if it's virtual. But it actually builds accountability because it makes clear that you care about the person's success, not just their productivity.

When employees know their manager cares about their wellbeing and clarity, they hold themselves accountable. They communicate problems before they become crises. They ask for help when they need it. They perform.

Surveillance doesn't create any of that. It creates the opposite.

4. Build Trust as a Two-Way Street, Backed by Policy and Practice

Trust in hybrid work isn't theoretical. It has to be structural.

On the employee side, this means:

- Clear role definitions and success metrics
- Transparent communication about company direction and their place in it
- Fair evaluation processes that don't penalize remote work
- Career development opportunities despite hybrid status

On the organizational side, this means:

- Protecting job security and not using hybrid status as a pretext for cuts
- Fair compensation and overtime practices
- Respecting work boundaries and not expecting constant availability
- Investing in tools and infrastructure that make remote work functional

When both sides are met, accountability becomes possible. Employees know what's expected. They know they won't be punished for boundaries. They know career progression isn't limited to visible presence. They know their company is invested in their success.

In return, they deliver. Not because they're monitored. Because they're trusted and they know it.

The Uncomfortable Conversation

This chapter requires acknowledging something many leaders don't want to face: **the accountability crisis in hybrid work isn't primarily a management problem. It's a systems problem.**

Your managers didn't suddenly become bad at accountability when people started working from home. The measuring sticks just changed. The visibility disappeared. And instead of investing in new approaches—outcome focus, clear metrics, regular communication—many organizations reached for the easiest tool: surveillance.

That's a choice. And it comes with costs that aren't visible in the first quarter.

High-performing employees leave organizations that surveil them. They work somewhere that trusts them. The talent market is making that clear.

Companies that build genuine accountability systems—clear outcomes, transparent evaluation, policy-backed protection, empathy-led management—outperform those that rely on surveillance. Not just on employee satisfaction metrics. On actual business outcomes.

The teams that trust each other move faster. They communicate better. They catch problems earlier. They collaborate more effectively across distance.

Surveillance does the opposite. It slows everything down. It creates defensive communication. It makes people protect turf instead of solve problems.

What Needs to Change in Leadership Mindset

Stop conflating visibility with accountability. They're not the same thing. Visibility is easier to measure, which is why leaders gravitate toward it. But it's not what creates high performance in distributed work.

Accountability comes from clarity. It comes from trust. It comes from aligned outcomes and regular feedback. It's harder to build. It requires more skill. But it actually works.

In Organizational Policy

Hybrid work creates complexity. Respond with clarity, not control.

- Define what done looks like for each role
- Create transparent performance evaluation frameworks
- Establish and protect work-hour boundaries
- Ensure fair compensation practices
- Make career advancement possible regardless of work location
- Invest in the tools and infrastructure that make hybrid work functional

In Labour and Regulatory Engagement

This is the one that requires courage.

If you're operating in environments where labour protections are eroding—where layoff thresholds are rising, where workday limits are expanding without compensation, where flexibility is becoming a liability—you have a voice in those conversations.

Use it. Not out of altruism, but out of enlightened self-interest. Weakened labour protections don't protect businesses. They create instability. They weaken trust. They make it harder for you to attract and retain the talent you need.

The best organizations are already doing this. They're advocating for policy that protects hybrid workers. They're not waiting for labour movements to force their hand. They're getting ahead of it because they understand: you can't build accountability on a foundation of fear.

The Real Accountability Question

Here's what it comes down to:

Are you trying to *control* people, or are you trying to *enable* them?

If you're trying to control them, surveillance and presence management make sense. But you'll never get genuine accountability. You'll get compliance. And compliance in a distributed workforce is the minimum. It's not excellence.

If you're trying to enable them, you invest in clarity, trust, and protection. You do harder work as a manager. You engage with policy questions that affect your workforce. You build systems that reward outcomes instead of visibility.

That path is harder. But it's the only path to accountability that actually works in the hybrid era.

The Path Forward

This isn't about being soft on performance. It's about being smart about it.

Accountability in hybrid work is built on:

1. Clear outcome definitions
2. Transparent measurement
3. Regular, honest feedback
4. Policy-backed protection
5. Leadership empathy
6. Organizational investment

Get that right, and you don't need surveillance. Your people hold themselves accountable because they trust you, they understand what success looks like, and they know you're invested in their success.

That's the hybrid era accountability that actually works.

And it starts with recognizing a simple truth: **you can't demand accountability from people you don't trust. And you can't expect trust from people you surveil.**

The choice is yours. But the market will tell you which approach works.

11

Measuring What Really Matters in R&D

The Measurement Trap

We measure OTD. On-time delivery. We track FTR—first-time right rates. We obsess over uptime, success rates, cycle time, defect density. We have dashboards for everything.

And our R&D teams are still burned out, disengaged, and leaving.

No metric matters if your team isn't driven by purpose, focused on the right goals, or truly committed to the mission. You can hit every technical KPI and still lose the innovation that makes R&D matter.

The problem isn't that we're measuring too much. It's that we're measuring the wrong things.

Why Technical KPIs Aren't Enough

Here's what traditional R&D metrics capture: output. What did we deliver? How fast did we deliver it? How many defects did we find? These are important. But they're incomplete.

They don't tell you why people are delivering it. They don't tell you if the team understands why it matters. They don't tell you if people are staying because they're engaged or because they haven't found a way out. They don't tell you if innovation is flourishing or if it's being systematically crushed under the weight of execution pressure.

Traditional metrics are rearview mirrors. They show you where you've been. They don't show you where you're headed—especially the human trajectory. And that's where real problems emerge.

A team that hits all its technical targets while losing its best people is failing. A team that nails every deadline while grinding through burnout is failing. A team that executes flawlessly while people arc just going through the motions is failing, even if nobody can see it yet in the numbers.

You see it later, when retention drops. When innovation slows. When the culture that built your competitive advantage has eroded.

Three Human-Centered KPIs That Actually Matter

1. Purpose Alignment

"I feel my work contributes to something meaningful."
This is the foundation. Without it, nothing else matters.

In R&D, purpose alignment is what separates people who show up to solve problems from people who show up to collect pay checks. It's the difference between a team that's building something and a team that's executing someone else's vision.

How to measure it:
Simple pulse surveys. Not elaborate engagement surveys. Just quarterly or bi-annual questions:

- "I understand how my work connects to our business strategy."
- "I can explain our mission to someone outside the company."
- "My current work aligns with what I find meaningful."
- "I see how my contributions matter to our customers/users."

Track the trend. A declining purpose alignment score is an early warning signal that something's wrong before attrition shows up in your turnover metrics.

Why it matters:

Purpose fuels innovation. When people understand why they're solving a problem—not just what the requirements are, but *why it matters*—they think differently. They bring ideas you didn't ask for. They push back on solutions that don't fit the mission. They go the extra mile because they're invested, not because they're managed.

The hard truth:

I tried implementing this in my team, and it was genuinely difficult. Top-down demands bring you face-to-face with organizational realities. You can't mandate purpose. You can only create the conditions for it to exist.

If your organization's messaging is mixed—if you say innovation matters but you're cutting investment, if you say people matter but you're grinding through layoffs, if you say quality matters but you're pressuring speed—your purpose alignment score will tell you that clearly. It will reflect the gap between what you say and what people experience.

That's not a measurement problem. That's a leadership problem. But at least you'll see it.

2. Strategic Focus Ratio

How many of your team's active initiatives actually move the needle?

This isn't about being busy. It's about being aligned with impactful work.

Most R&D teams are drowning in tasks. They're juggling core delivery, bug fixes, technical debt, maintenance work, and ad-hoc requests. Meanwhile, the strategic initiatives that could actually transform the product or business are perpetually "next quarter."

The Strategic Focus Ratio asks: Of all the work your team is doing, what percentage directly advances your strategic priorities?

How to measure it:

Categorize your team's active work:

- **Strategic initiatives** (directly supporting 3-5 year goals)
- **Core delivery** (essential maintenance and support)

- **Technical debt and infrastructure** (necessary but not strategic)
- **Reactive and ad-hoc** (interrupts and unplanned work)

Calculate what percentage of team capacity is actually going to strategic work.

What's realistic:

If you're being honest, most teams operate at 20-30% strategic focus. Your best teams might hit 50%. The 20% figure is possible, but it requires discipline, clear prioritization, and willingness to say no.

Why it matters:

Strategic focus is where innovation happens. When your team is fragmented across dozens of competing priorities, nobody has the bandwidth to think deeply, experiment safely, or build something transformational. You get incremental improvements and maintenance execution.

But when you can concentrate meaningful capacity on strategic work, you unlock R&D's actual purpose. You build products and capabilities that move the business forward, not just keep the lights on.

The constraint:

All team members are too core-focused. That's the reality. Your team carries essential work that can't be delegated away. But here's the choice: you can either acknowledge that constraint and protect strategic work ruthlessly, or you can pretend it doesn't exist while your strategic initiatives never get the focus they need.

Most teams choose the latter. Then they wonder why innovation feels stalled.

3. Discretionary Effort Index

Are people just ticking boxes, or are they going the extra mile because they care?

This is the hardest metric to measure, but it's often the most revealing.

Discretionary effort shows up in ways you can observe: voluntary ideas in team meetings, someone staying late to solve a problem (not because they were told to, but because they cared), cross-team collaboration that goes beyond requirements, people suggesting improvements instead of just executing them.

It also shows up in ways you can't always see: the mental energy someone brings to problem-solving, the quality of thinking in design reviews, the depth of ownership people takes for outcomes.

When discretionary effort is high, your team punches above its weight. People bring their whole selves to work. They're invested in quality, not just completion. They think strategically about decisions, not just tactically.

When discretionary effort is low, you get compliance. Tasks complete. Deliverables ship. But nothing exceptional happens. Your team becomes average, even if individually talented.

How to measure it:

This requires observation, not just surveys. Look for:

- Are people volunteering ideas in meetings, or just implementing?
- Are there cross-team initiatives beyond assigned scope?
- Do people push back thoughtfully on decisions, or just accept them?
- Are there internal mentoring and knowledge-sharing happening organically?
- Are people staying engaged during slower periods, or just going through the motions?

Then ask directly in 1-on-1s: "Do you feel like you're bringing your best thinking to this work, or are you operating on fumes?"

The real challenge:

As teams get saturated—and most R&D teams are saturated—discretionary effort becomes a real drag. People have nothing left to give. They're managing at capacity just to stay afloat.

You need to be a genuinely inspiring leader to make this happen under pressure. You can't manufacture discretionary effort. You can only create the conditions where people still have something left after they've delivered their core work.

That means: reasonable workloads. Clear priorities. Psychological safety to think beyond immediate tasks. Recognition for ideas and ownership. Space for learning and growth.

Without those conditions, expecting discretionary effort is asking people to give you extra while you've already taken their maximum.

Building an Engaged Execution Index

These three KPIs individually matter. But together, they form something more powerful: an **Engaged Execution Index**.

This is a composite view of how well your team is functioning as a human system, not just a delivery system.

The formula is simple:

Engaged Execution Index = Purpose Alignment + Strategic Focus + Discretionary Effort

Track each component. Then look at the aggregate.

A team with high purpose, strong strategic focus, and discretionary effort is performing at its potential. They're innovating. They're sustainable. They're producing quality.

A team with high purpose but scattered focus is passionate but ineffective. They care deeply but feel like they're failing because their work is fragmented.

A team with strong focus but low purpose is grinding. They're hitting targets but losing soul. Attrition will follow.

A team with low discretionary effort across all three is in trouble. They're not engaged, they're not aligned, and they're not focused. Your retention, innovation, and quality will all suffer.

How to Use This Data

Measuring these KPIs is useless if you don't act on them.

Talk about it openly

Bring these metrics into your team meetings. Share the results. Ask people what they see in the data. What's driving low purpose alignment? What's fragmenting focus? What would make people bring more discretionary effort?

Don't make it feel like evaluation. Make it feel like diagnosis. You're looking at the health of the team together, and you're asking: what needs to change?

Improve it with intention.

If purpose alignment is dropping, that's not a communication problem you can solve with one town hall. It's a signal that something in your strategy, your messaging, or your execution isn't landing. Dig into that.

If strategic focus is low, stop adding initiatives. Kill something. Tell people no. Create space.

If discretionary effort is fading, look at workload, burnout, and psychological safety. You can't shame people into caring more. You have to remove the barriers to caring.

The Uncomfortable Truth

This chapter requires acknowledging something most R&D leaders don't want to face: **you've been optimizing for the wrong things.**

Not deliberately. The metrics industry has given you—OTD, FTR, cycle time, defect rates—are valuable. But they're metrics of *execution*, not metrics of *excellence*.

You can execute flawlessly and still have a mediocre team that's not innovating, not learning, not pushing boundaries. And you can miss that completely if you're only looking at technical metrics.

The organizations that are winning in R&D aren't winning because they deliver faster. They're winning because their teams are engaged, aligned, and thinking deeply about hard problems.

Those teams deliver better outcomes not in spite of being human-centered, but because of it.

The Path Forward

This isn't about replacing technical KPIs. It's about completing the picture.

Start tracking Purpose Alignment, Strategic Focus, and Discretionary Effort alongside your technical metrics.

Build your Engaged Execution Index. Make it visible. Talk about it quarterly. Let it guide your decisions about workload, priorities, and culture.

Because here's the simple truth: **continuous improvement starts with your people. Not your process.**

Your processes are only as good as the people executing them. And your people are only as capable as they are engaged, focused, and motivated.

Get that right, and everything else gets easier.

The metrics will tell you when it's working.

Questions for Your Leadership

- What percentage of your team's work is actually strategic? Would you want to know?
- If you asked your team "Do you feel your work is meaningful?" tomorrow, what would they say? Would the answer surprise you?
- Are people bringing their best thinking, or are they managing to survive?
- What would need to change for you to protect 20-30% of team capacity for strategic work?
- If discretionary effort is low, what's actually the barrier? Workload? Clarity? Inspiration? Something else?

The answers to these questions matter more than hitting any technical deadline.

Because the teams that are building the future aren't the ones optimizing for today. They're the ones that are energized, aligned, and thinking long-term.

That starts with measuring what really matters.

12

The Technical Leadership Gap

The Invisible Failure

Technically sound leaders often lose their edge the moment they step into senior leadership roles. Not because they forget their domain knowledge. Not because they stop understanding the work. But because they start delegating without context—pushing their subject matter experts into unstructured, ambiguous situations that demand leadership, not just execution.

And the experts feel it immediately.

They recognize it as: "My leader doesn't have time to think this through." Or worse: "My leader doesn't trust me to understand the full problem." What they experience is being asked to solve something they can't fully see. Being handed a piece of a puzzle without knowing what the picture is supposed to be.

That's demoralizing. And it's a silent competence killer.

The Context Problem: A Real Example

I was involved in a strategic discussion on variant reduction in automotive interiors—a critical area where even the smallest change requires deep understanding of cabin architecture, user interaction zones, manufacturing constraints, and customer expectations.

The situation seemed straightforward: we needed to make a decision, and it needed to be made quickly.

The challenge? I didn't have a full-cabin expert immediately available. What I had instead were multiple team members with strong yet fragmented knowledge. One person understood structural integration. Another understood user ergonomics. Another had deep manufacturing expertise. Another knew the supply chain implications.

The lazy move would have been obvious: hand the problem to whoever seemed most senior and ask them to figure it out. They probably could have. They're capable. They're smart. They'd deliver something.

But would that be wise? No.

Here's why: By delegating to a single person without first building context myself, I would have been:

1. **Forcing them to become the context-builder** instead of the solution-provider. They'd spend energy connecting dots that I could connect. They'd make assumptions about priorities without knowing which trade-offs matter most to the business.
2. **Creating misalignment risk.** Different team members would interpret the problem differently. Some would optimize for cost. Others for user experience. Others for supply chain efficiency. Without unified context about what we were actually optimizing for, they'd pull in different directions.
3. **Demotivating the exact people, I needed most.** By throwing an ambiguous problem at experts, I'd be signalling: "You figure it out." That's not leadership. That's abdication. And experts recognize it immediately.
4. **Missing the real value I could add as a leader.** My team members could each solve their piece brilliantly. But what only I could do was connect those pieces into a coherent strategy.

What I Did Instead

I took ownership of the ambiguity myself—first.

I framed the problem:

1. What exactly are we trying to solve? Not "reduce variants," but specifically: which variants create the most manufacturing complexity without delivering customer value?
2. What are the constraints? Cost targets, timeline, supply chain dependencies, regulatory requirements.
3. What are the trade-offs? If we prioritize cost reduction, what customer experience gets compromised? If we prioritize engineering simplicity, where does that hurt manufacturing?

I built the context:

1. I brought together the fragmented expertise in the room and connected it into a coherent picture. I helped people see how their piece fit into the whole.
2. I shared what I knew about business priorities, customer feedback, and strategic direction—information that team members might not have access to.
3. I made visible the decision criteria: what success actually looks like, not just from a technical standpoint, but from a business standpoint.

I defined the constraints:

1. Timeline: when does this decision need to be made?
2. Resource availability: who can focus on this, and for how long?
3. Scope boundaries: what's in scope for this discussion, and what's out?
4. Escalation points: if we hit a trade-off we can't resolve, where does it go?

Only then did I mobilize the team.

With that foundation, the experts could operate at full capacity. They understood what problem we were solving. They knew the constraints. They could make intelligent trade-offs because they understood the priorities. And they could work together instead of in silos.

That's the difference between delegating a problem and leading people to solve it.

Why Context Matters More Than You Think

When leaders skip the context-building phase, they create several problems simultaneously:

The Misalignment Problem

Experts make decisions based on what they optimize for. Without clear context, different experts optimize for different things. Your structural engineer optimizes for simplicity. Your manufacturing engineer optimizes for cost. Your user experience expert optimizes for capability. They're all right—but they're solving different problems.

Then you have to resolve the conflicts, which means rework, delays, and frustration from people who thought they were solving the right problem.

With context: everyone is optimizing for the same outcome because they understand why that outcome matters.

The Assumption Problem

When ambiguity exists, people fill it with assumptions. And those assumptions are often invisible until something breaks.

Your expert might assume cost is the primary driver. So, they design a solution that sacrifices user experience. Then leadership says, "That's not what we needed." The expert feels blindsided. The leader feels like the expert misunderstood priorities. Frustration on both sides.

With context: the priorities are explicit. Assumptions are made visible and discussed upfront.

The Motivation Problem

Experts are motivated by solving interesting, well-defined problems. Give them an ambiguous mess without context, and you're asking them to be problem-definers, not problem-solvers. That's not their job. And more importantly, it's exhausting.

They're spending energy on the wrong thing. Instead of bringing their expertise to bear on a clear challenge, they're trying to figure out what the challenge actually is.

With context: they can focus their expertise where it matters. They feel respected because you've done your job as a leader.

How to Lead Experts Smarter Than You

This is where the technical leadership gap becomes acute. Many leaders reach a point where they're leading people with deeper technical expertise than they have. And that creates a specific anxiety: *How do I lead someone I can't out-think on their domain?*

The answer is counterintuitive: **you lead them by not trying.**

You Can't Out-Expert Them. Don't Try.

If you're leading a mechanical engineer and they have 15 years of automotive experience and you have 8, you will lose a technical depth competition. Stop trying to win it.

Your role isn't to be smarter than them technically. Your role is to be smarter about context, priorities, and trade-offs.

You Lead Through Context, Not Through Technical Direction

Here's what you *can* do that they can't:

- See across domains. They see their corner. You see how their work connects to five other teams.
- Understand business context. They understand the technical problem. You understand why the business cares.
- Hold space for ambiguity while it becomes clarity. They're expert at solving defined problems. You're responsible for defining the problem in the first place.

- Make trade-off decisions. They can tell you the technical implications. You have to decide what's actually worth the trade.

This is where your value as a leader lives. Not in being more technical. But in being more *contextual.*

The Mistake Leaders Make

Many leaders who are leading experts smarter than they are respond with one of two mistakes:

Mistake 1: Over-directing technically. They try to maintain authority by making technical decisions. This signals to the expert: "I don't trust your judgment." It wastes the expert's capability. And it's usually wrong because the leader doesn't have enough depth to make good technical calls.

Mistake 2: Under-leading entirely. They step back and say "You're the expert, figure it out." This abdicates the leadership role. The expert ends up doing both their job and the leader's job. They get frustrated. And strategic direction gets lost because nobody's connecting the dots.

The right move is something different.

Leading Experts Smarter Than You

1. Get clear on what you actually know.

Don't pretend to technical expertise you don't have. But do bring what you know: business priorities, strategic direction, competitive context, customer feedback, organizational constraints.

Be explicit: "Here's what I understand about the business direction. Here's what I know about our constraints. I'm going to rely on your technical judgment on the details. But I need you to help me understand the trade-offs so I can make the right calls."

That's credible. That's honest. And that's actually what experts respect.

2. Own the ambiguity.

You're responsible for the part that's unclear. Not because you need to solve it technically, but because you need to bring clarity to it.

For your expert, this might mean: "I know what the end goal is, but I need to understand the path better. Help me see the options and the implications so I can make an informed decision."

You're asking them to educate you—not so you can become an expert, but so you can be a better leader.

3. Create space for their expertise to flourish.

Give them clear problems to solve. Remove obstacles. Get them the resources they need. Make sure organizational politics don't derail their work. Advocate for their ideas in rooms where they're not present.

This is where your authority actually matters. You can't out-think them. But you can remove friction from their work and amplify their impact.

4. Push back on fuzzy thinking—including their own.

Just because they're the expert doesn't mean they're always right about everything. Sometimes experts get lost in technical depth and lose sight of business reality. Or they optimize for perfect engineering and miss practical constraints.

Your role is to ask: "I hear why this is the right solution technically. Help me understand why it's the right solution for our business right now?"

This isn't second-guessing their expertise. This is holding them accountable to outcomes, not just technical elegance.

5. Make the leadership decisions they can't make.

They can tell you the technical implications. You decide what's worth it. You decide which trade-offs to take. You decide when "good enough" is actually good enough. You decide when to push back on timelines and when to respect them.

These aren't technical decisions. But they're critical leadership decisions. And only you can make them—not because you're smarter, but because you're responsible for outcomes across the organization, not just within one domain.

The Real Competence You Need

There's a specific competence that separates good technical leaders from great ones. It's not about being the smartest person in the room technically.

It's about being the person who:

- Can see the whole problem clearly enough to frame it
- Can connect fragmented expertise into coherent strategy
- Can hold ambiguity without dumping it on experts
- Can make trade-off decisions because they understand context
- Can lead people smarter than they are by creating conditions for those experts to excel

This competence is rare. And it's what separates leaders who amplify their team's capabilities from leaders who inadvertently suppress them.

The Critical Mistake

Here's what many leaders miss: **delegating a problem without context isn't efficiency. It's abdication.**

It *feels* efficient. You hand off work and the expert gets to work. But you've actually created waste:

- Waste of the expert's time trying to figure out what they're solving
- Waste of misaligned efforts that will need rework
- Waste of expertise that could have been better deployed with clearer direction
- Waste of team motivation when people feel their leader isn't doing their job

Real efficiency looks different. It looks like: invest time upfront in framing, context, and clarity. Then the expert can operate at full speed without wasted motion.

The Path Forward: Using Experts Wisely

Don't just delegate. Lead.

Before you hand off a problem:

- Have you framed it clearly enough that the expert understands not just what, but why?
- Have you provided the business context they need to make good trade-offs?
- Have you defined the constraints and decision criteria?
- Have you connected this work to the bigger strategic picture?
- Have you removed organizational obstacles that might slow them down?

As they work:

- Are they operating at full expertise, or are they burning energy on ambiguity?
- Do they feel trusted, or do they feel like they're being managed?
- Are they making progress, or are they spinning on clarification?

With the results:

- Did they solve the right problem?
- Did they understand the trade-offs they were making?
- Could they explain their decision to someone outside their domain?

The Insight That Changes Everything

You don't hire experts so you can manage their work better. You hire experts so they can bring their best thinking to problems that matter.

But they can only do that if you first create the clarity, context, and strategic direction they need.

Leadership isn't delegation. It's the work you do before delegation so that delegation actually works.

Context before delegation. Strategy before execution. Clarity before complexity.

Get that right, and you don't need to be smarter than your experts. You just need to be the leader they deserve.

And that's a different—and much more valuable—kind of competence.

Part – IV

Inner Leadership: Mind-set & Reflection

13

When Do You Give Up?

The Question That Never Stops

When do you give up? It's a question that doesn't announce itself once and disappear. It's not a problem you solve in your early career and then move past. Instead, it returns—regularly, persistently, at different intervals throughout your leadership journey, always timed perfectly to test whether you're still in the game.

Most leaders expect failure to be something they outgrow. We imagine that once we achieve a certain level of success, once we've "made it," the question of quitting will stop haunting us. But that's not how it works. The multi-loop of failures doesn't end. Success keeps eluding you in new ways, through different challenges, across different contexts. And each time, the same question resurfaces: *Should I give up?*

The Game Never Truly Ends

Here's what I've learned: if you do give up, the game doesn't end. You simply join another game—maybe a different one, in a different industry or role or venture. But here's the catch—you'll face this situation again. The fundamental struggle doesn't disappear; it just reshapes itself. You're not escaping the question; you're just changing the arena in which you encounter it.

This is both sobering and liberating. It's sobering because it means there's no permanent finish line where the struggle stops. It's liberating because it means the decision to give up now isn't actually a decision to be done with struggle—it's just a decision to struggle somewhere else.

The real question, then, isn't "Will I face failure again?" The answer to that is yes, inevitably. The real question becomes: "Am I clear about my path? Do I feel strongly about this direction?"

Failure Doesn't Justify Quitting

Truly successful individuals aren't the ones who never fail. They're the ones who fail repeatedly and keep at it anyway. This distinction matters deeply.

Failure is information. Failure is feedback. Failure is part of the process. But failure is not permission to quit—not if you're still clear about your direction, not if you still feel strongly about the path ahead.

When you're in the thick of it—when the failures mount, when success seems to recede no matter what you do—clarity and conviction become your compass. Not optimism. Not blind faith. Not magical thinking. Clarity about *why* you're doing this, and conviction that you haven't abandoned the true path.

If you feel strongly and are clear of the path, then the answer is: just keep walking on it.

The Milestone around the Corner

This isn't naive persistence. It's not about grinding endlessly toward an illusion. It's about recognizing something crucial: you may not see the milestone yet. It may be just at the next corner. The breakthrough could be one more attempt away, one more pivot away, one more conversation away.

But here's what you'll never know if you give up: whether you were right all along.

That unknowing is perhaps the heaviest burden a leader carries. Not the struggle itself—the wondering afterward. The persistent question: *Was I actually on the right path? Would it have worked if I'd just kept going?*

Some leaders can live with that. Some can give up and move forward without that weight. But most of us can't. Most of us know, in our gut, whether we were tracking toward something real or chasing an illusion. And if there's even a chance we were on the right path, the decision to quit becomes harder to live with than the decision to persist.

The Psychological Journey

This is the psychological heart of resilience—not the ability to absorb punishment, but the clarity to distinguish between a worthy struggle and a lost cause, and the conviction to keep going when the answer isn't obvious.

Resilience isn't optimism. It's not pretending things are better than they are. True resilience is the ability to keep moving forward while fully acknowledging how hard it is, while sitting with the uncertainty of whether it will work, while accepting that failure might come again.

It's knowing the game will continue. It's understanding that giving up doesn't end struggle; it just relocates it. And it's choosing to stay in *this* game, *this* path, because you believe in it and you haven't reached the corner yet.

The leadership journey doesn't end the question "When do you give up?" It teaches you to ask a better one: "Should I?"

14

From Burnout to Breakthrough

The Lowest Point

A few years ago, I found myself at one of the lowest points in my career. The pressure was relentless—not the kind that sharpens you, but the kind that wears you down. Negative thoughts weren't occasional visitors; they were constant residents. My biggest battle wasn't about strategy or execution or market competition. It was simply about staying true to the professional I had always strived to be.

When you're depleted, even being yourself feels like climbing a mountain.

I was still showing up. I was still performing. But something essential had drained away—the sense that any of it mattered, that I was moving toward something, that growth was still possible. I was going through the motions while the person I wanted to be seemed increasingly unreachable.

That's when I saw an ad for the Executive MBA program at SIMS.

My first instinct was doubt. *Another commitment? More pressure? More work?* I was already stretched thin. But something else whispered louder: *What if this is exactly what you need?*

The Permission to Pause and Redirect

The initial assessment and personal interview with, the Deputy Director and Course Coordinator @ SIMS, changed everything. It wasn't a sales pitch. It was a genuine conversation—someone who understood what real transformation looked like, who could see past my exhaustion to what might be possible.

That conversation gave me permission. Permission to redirect my energy. Permission to step back and rebuild myself intentionally, rather than continuing to deteriorate in place.

I took the plunge.

The Sanctuary

What followed were 2.5 of the most intense and rewarding years of my life. Every weekend, from 10 AM to 6 PM, I committed fully. No excuses. No missed classes. Just a deep desire to learn, grow, and rediscover my passion.

Here's what surprised me: the classroom became my sanctuary. Not a burden. A sanctuary.

In a world where everything felt fragmented and uncertain, the program gave me structure. When my professional life felt chaotic, the rigor of learning became grounding. When I was losing faith in myself, encountering new ideas and perspectives reminded me that growth was still possible.

The program became my stress buster—not because it was easy, but because it was intentional. Every weekend was a choice I was making toward something rather than away from something. That distinction matters profoundly when you're recovering from burnout.

Learning as Therapy

There's a reason therapy often involves learning to see your situation differently. The Executive MBA did that, but through the lens of business, leadership, strategy, and human behaviour. Every subject—organizational psychology, strategic thinking, economics, ethics, operations—became a lens through which I could reexamine my own journey.

I wasn't just acquiring knowledge. I was processing trauma through frameworks. I was rebuilding confidence through competence. I was rediscovering my own agency in conversations with peers who were fighting their own battles.

The professors didn't just teach content; they modelled what it looks like to think deeply, to question assumptions, to stay curious even in complexity. My colleagues weren't just classmates; they were mirrors reflecting back my own struggles and reminding me I wasn't alone.

In learning with others who were also searching for something, I found community. In mastering new concepts, I found efficacy. In committing to something beyond my immediate crisis, I found purpose rekindling.

The Journey of Transformation

The transformation wasn't instantaneous. It was gradual—built on weekends, on conversations, on the discipline of showing up even when you don't feel like it. It was built on the decision that this 2.5-year investment in myself mattered more than the extra hours I could have worked, the meetings I could have taken, the reactive scrambling I could have done.

Looking back, I see how burnout had narrowed my world. I was trapped in a single loop of pressure and performance. The program widened my perspective. It reminded me that leadership isn't just about surviving the current crisis—it's about understanding yourself, understanding systems, understanding people.

Today, I look back with immense gratitude to my course professors, colleagues, and friends. Not just for the degree, but for the resilience, discipline, and confidence it helped me reclaim. They became the community that held me accountable to becoming myself again.

When you're in a Tough Place

If you're ever at a low point—mentally, emotionally, or professionally—remember this: sometimes the best way out isn't to push harder. It isn't to grip tighter to what you're doing.

Sometimes the best way out is to lean in. Lean into learning. Lean into growth. Lean into community. Lean into the things that reconnect you with why you became a leader in the first place.

Burnout often stems from a sense of being trapped—trapped by circumstances, by expectations, by your own identity as "someone who pushes through." Breaking that trap doesn't require you to quit. It requires you to redirect your energy toward something that reminds you who you are and what you're capable of becoming.

The breakthrough came not from solving the immediate problem, but from stepping outside it long enough to remember that I was bigger than my current crisis. That there was more to discover. That learning was still possible. That I could rebuild.

The classroom saved me—not because it was an escape, but because it was a path forward.

The Resilience Within

What I reclaimed through that journey wasn't just a degree. It was the understanding that resilience isn't about never breaking. Resilience is about having the wisdom to know when you need help, the courage to invest in yourself, and the discipline to show up—even when everything in you wants to give up.

Sometimes the most powerful leadership move you can make is the decision to become a student again.

15
The Ego Trap

The Line Where Leadership Ends

The moment ego replaces accountability, leadership ends.

That's not a gradual decline. That's not something that happens over time if you're not careful. That's a cliff edge—and many leaders walk right off it without realizing they've crossed the threshold.

I've spent 25 years in the automotive interiors industry, and in that time, I've watched careers. I've watched decisions play out. I've watched leaders rise and fall. And the pattern is unmistakable: the ones who stay are the ones who never let ego replace accountability. The ones who fall are the ones who do.

This isn't about whether you make mistakes. Every leader makes mistakes. The question is what you do when you make them.

The Fear That Separates Great Leaders

Great leaders—and I'll be honest; there are very few of them—don't fear mistakes. This might surprise you. It's not that they don't make errors in judgment or strategic miscalculations. Of course they do.

What they fear is missed responsibility.

There's a profound difference. A mistake is something that happened. Missed responsibility is something you caused to happen by not owning it.

When a decision goes wrong, a leader with ego will:

- Find someone else to blame
- Reframe what happened to make it look better
- Defend the decision rather than learn from it
- Protect their image of infallibility

When a decision goes wrong, a leader with humility will:

- Acknowledge what happened clearly
- Ask what they could have done differently
- Extract the lesson
- Use it to lead differently next time

One protects the past. The other builds the future.

Staying Humble Under Pressure

Here's where most leaders fail: humility is easy when things are going well. It's effortless to be modest when success is flowing. The real test comes under pressure—when your job might be on the line, when a major decision has backfired, when your credibility is being questioned.

That's when ego whispers: *Defend yourself. Prove you're right. Show them they're wrong to doubt you.*

And that's when humility becomes a choice rather than a luxury. That's when it separates the leaders who build long-term credibility from the ones who sacrifice their future for momentary protection.

Staying humble under pressure means:

- Admitting uncertainty when you feel it
- Asking for input when you don't have all the answers
- Changing course when the evidence suggests you should
- Crediting others when things go well
- Owning failures without excuse or spin

This isn't weakness. It's the opposite. It takes far more strength to say "I was wrong" under pressure than to defend a failing position. It takes more courage to admit what you don't know than to pretend expertise you don't possess.

Why Ego-Driven Decisions Rarely Survive Scrutiny

Think about the decisions that have caused the most damage in organizations—the ones that people still talk about years later, that destroyed morale, that cost money or relationships or market position.

Usually, there's an ego decision at the center.

An ego-driven decision is one that prioritizes the leader's need to be right, to be seen as visionary, to be proven correct—over what's actually best for the organization or the people involved.

Ego decisions survive internal discussions fine. They can sound compelling in the moment. They can rally people behind a charismatic vision. But they rarely survive real-world scrutiny. When you run them up against complexity, against resistance, against actual outcomes, they tend to crumble.

Why? Because they weren't built on sound reasoning. They were built on the need to satisfy an ego.

Accountable decisions, by contrast, can survive scrutiny because they're rooted in:

- Clear thinking about trade-offs
- Honest assessment of risks
- Genuine consideration of alternatives
- Willingness to be wrong
- Focus on outcomes rather than image

The 25-Year Pattern

After a quarter-century in this industry, I've seen enough cycles to recognize the pattern. The leaders who are still respected, still trusted, still effective—they're not the smartest people in the room. They're not the ones with the most degrees or the most impressive résumés.

They're the ones who own their decisions. The ones who say, "I made that call, and here's what I learned from it." The ones who can be challenged without becoming defensive. The ones who can say "I don't know" without it diminishing their authority.

I've also seen the other kind—the ones who were brilliant once but whose careers stalled or crashed. Almost always, it was the same story: ego took over. They stopped listening. They stopped learning. They started protecting their image instead of pursuing what was right.

And their teams knew it. Their peers knew it. Eventually, the market knew it.

Accountability as the True Mark of Leadership

Here's what I've come to understand: leadership isn't about having all the answers. It's not about being the smartest person in the room or having the most experience or making decisions that always turn out right.

Leadership is about being accountable. It's about creating an environment where people know that if something goes wrong, their leader will own it. Where mistakes are information, not career-ending disasters. Where the focus is on learning and improving, not on protecting reputations.

When accountability replaces ego, everything changes. Teams become more honest. Decisions improve. Mistakes get caught earlier. Innovation accelerates because people aren't afraid to take smart risks.

The moment ego replaces accountability is the moment you stop being a leader. You might still have the title. You might still have the authority. But you've lost the thing that actually makes leadership work: the trust that comes from knowing your leader will do the right thing, even when it's hard.

The Long-Term Advantage

Humility isn't about self-deprecation. It's not about downplaying your achievements or pretending you don't have value to contribute. Real humility is knowing exactly what you bring to the table and being secure enough not to exaggerate it or defend it unnecessarily.

Leaders with genuine humility have a long-term advantage because:

- People trust them more, because trust isn't based on image—it's based on consistency
- They learn faster, because they're not defending past decisions, they're extracting lessons from them
- They attract better people, because strong people want to work for leaders who don't need to dominate
- They make better decisions, because they're willing to challenge their own thinking
- They survive scrutiny, because their decisions are built on substance, not ego

The ego trap looks tempting in the moment. It feels good to defend your position, to be seen as unshakable, to project confidence that borders on certainty. But that feeling is temporary. The damage is long-term.

The leader who can stay humble under pressure, who can own mistakes without excuse, who can shift from "I'm right" to "What's right?"—that's the leader who builds something that lasts.

That's the leader people follow not because they have to, but because they want to.

The Choice

Every day, leaders face the choice: protect ego or pursue accountability. Defend the past or build the future. Be right or be effective.

After 25 years, I know which choice separates the leaders who last from the ones who don't.

The ego trap isn't something you fall into once and then avoid forever. It's a constant temptation, especially as you gain success and authority. The protection against it isn't willpower or self-awareness alone.

It's remembering, again and again, that the moment you choose ego over accountability is the moment you stop being a leader.

16

When Potential Meets Setbacks

The Toughest Test

One of the toughest yet most meaningful challenges as a leader is when you see clear potential in a team member—not just a gut feeling, not a hunch based on charm or charisma. Real, observable potential: solid work ethic, structured thinking, genuine intent to grow and contribute.

And then the results don't land.

This is where leadership gets tested in ways that matter. Not in the moments when everything is working, when your best people are delivering, when momentum is on your side. It's in this grey space, where potential is visible but performance is lacking, that you discover what kind of leader you actually are.

I've faced this more than once in my career. Each time, it's been a difficult call. Each time, I've had to sit with uncertainty. Because here's the truth: you might be right about what needs to happen next, or you might be wrong. There's rarely a clear signal in the moment.

The Temptation of the Quick Call

In the real world, results are what matter. Organizations don't survive on potential alone. They survive on delivery, execution, impact. So, there's a powerful temptation when potential and results diverge: conclude that maybe this individual isn't ready. Maybe they peaked early. Maybe you misread them. And the solution seems obvious, move on, find someone who can deliver now.

The pressure to make that call is real. It's quick. It's clean. It moves the problem off your plate.

But before you close that chapter, pause.

Understanding before Judgment

Here's what I've learned: results are just the surface of the story. Results are the outcome. What matters for a leader is understanding what created that outcome.

First, sit with them. Not to evaluate or judge, but to genuinely understand. What situations have they been through? What obstacles have they faced that you might not be fully aware of? What's happening in their work life, their head space, their approach?

Sometimes a team member who isn't delivering is drowning in self-doubt they haven't articulated. Sometimes they're facing a situation they've never encountered before and don't know how to navigate. Sometimes they're in the wrong role not because they lack capability, but because they lack context or confidence in this particular area.

Help them reflect. Ask them what they think could have been done differently. Don't tell them. Ask them. People with real potential often have insight into their own gaps—they just need someone to create space for that reflection. Sometimes they're harder on themselves than you would be.

Encourage them to seek feedback from peers. Your view of their performance is one lens. Their peers see them differently—they might see strengths you don't, or they might validate your concerns with examples. More importantly, peer feedback often lands differently. It can be less threatening, more specific, and sometimes more credible to them than feedback from their leader.

This isn't delegation of your responsibility as a leader. It's expanding the data you're working with before you make a consequential decision.

A Change of Context

Sometimes potential isn't being realized because the context is wrong.

Try a different project. The work they're struggling with might not be the right canvas for their strengths. A new project can illuminate capability that wasn't visible before. Sometimes people need a fresh angle to find their footing. Sometimes they need to see themselves succeeding in order to believe they can.

Shadow them with another lead. Pair them with someone who approaches problems differently, who has a different pace, who brings different energy. You might be surprised what emerges. Sometimes the issue isn't capability—it's that they're not seeing how to apply their capability in the current environment. A different working style can unlock something.

Yes, this takes time. Yes, it's an investment. Yes, it's not the quickest path to resolution.

The Leader's Real Dilemma

And here's where your judgment as a leader truly matters: only you can decide how much time you can afford to invest.

You have finite resources. You have other demands. You have team morale to consider. You have business results to deliver. The question isn't whether you should invest in everyone indefinitely. Of course you can't. The question is whether you've invested *enough* before you make a final call.

Acting too soon has a cost that isn't always visible in the moment. You might just lose a future star. You might be discarding someone who was one setback away from breakthrough. You might be removing a strong contributor who could have genuinely benefited your team if given time to find their rhythm.

But acting too late has a cost too. You tie up resources. You send a signal to the rest of your team about what underperformance looks like. You risk the person becoming more entrenched in failure rather than mobilized toward growth.

The tension is real. There's no formula. But there's a principle: be fair—to them, and to yourself.

The Difference between a Quick Call and the Right Call

Sometimes, leadership is not about making the quick call. It's about making the right one.

A quick call feels decisive. It feels like you're taking action. It feels like you're solving a problem.

But the right call takes longer. It requires you to sit with discomfort. It requires you to try approaches that might not work. It requires you to see the person, not just their performance metrics. It requires you to distinguish between someone who truly doesn't have the capability versus someone who hasn't yet found how to apply it.

The right call also acknowledges that sometimes, after genuine investment and real attempts at support, the answer is that this person isn't the right fit for this role. That's a valid conclusion—but it's only valid if it comes after real effort to understand, not before.

When the System Is the Problem

Here's where this gets more complex—and more important. Sometimes when you sit down and truly understand what's happening, you discover something unsettling: the gap between potential and results isn't about the individual's capability. It's about the system they're operating in.

I learned this the hard way. I had a promising individual on my team—different in his approach, thoughtful about process, genuinely good at engineering. He was a performer, but things consistently didn't work out. Project after project, the results lagged. The more I investigated, the more I discovered the real issue: his approach, though promising and potentially more efficient, didn't align with what our global partners wanted.

The partners' expectation was simple: follow the task as assigned. Don't think otherwise. Don't add value in ways they didn't ask for. Don't innovate.

This person wasn't someone who wanted to do an average job. He wanted to make things better, to solve problems more elegantly, to bring perspective. But every time he did, it created friction. Every time he suggested a different path, it generated reasons to prove him wrong—not because his approach was flawed, but because it was different.

His setbacks weren't failures of capability. They were collisions with organizational rigidity.

My conclusion: he had real potential. If our partners had the right mindset—one that welcomed different perspectives, that saw thinking as part of the job, that valued efficiency and innovation—we would have had better results. We would have had a genuine contributor thriving, not struggling.

But he was struggling because the system punished what made him valuable.

This is a critical insight for leaders: sometimes the person isn't the problem. Sometimes the context is.

What You're Actually Testing

When you face this situation, you're not just deciding about the team member's future. You're making a statement about what leadership means in your organization.

If you move people out quickly when results lag potential, you're signalling that potential doesn't matter—only immediate delivery. You're discouraging thinking. You're making people fearful of bringing perspective that differs from the status quo. You're optimizing for compliance over contribution.

If you invest in people when they stumble, if you try to understand before you judge, if you examine not just *their* performance but the *system* they're performing in—you're signalling that you see people as whole, that you believe in growth, that a bad quarter doesn't define someone's future. You're also signalling that sometimes the real leadership work is pushing back on systems that stifle potential.

Both have consequences. Both shape your culture.

The difference is profound: one culture develops people who follow orders. The other develops people who think, contribute, and innovate—and leaders who are brave enough to advocate for them when the system tries to suppress them.

The Leader's Real Work

This is the work that separates managers from leaders. A manager can enforce expectations and manage out underperformance. A leader can do that *and* can look beneath results to understand what's actually happening.

Can you see potential when results are hidden? Can you invest time when the outcome is uncertain? Can you make space for growth while still holding people accountable?

Can you be fair—truly fair—when fairness requires more than you initially want to give?

That's when potential meets setbacks. That's when a leader's real test begins.

And sometimes, after all that investment, the answer is still that this isn't the right role or the right fit. That's okay. You made the right call—not because it was quick, but because it was earned.

17

Zindagi Gulzar Hai

The Poetry and the Reality

"Zindagi Gulzar Hai." A beautiful phrase. It translates to "Life is a Garden" or "Life is Blooming." The words sound poetic, hopeful—almost naive when you're stuck in a cycle of constant struggle.

It's easy to sell the idea of a beautiful life when you're not the one carrying the weight. When you're not the one fighting. When exhaustion isn't a permanent condition and setbacks aren't a recurring pattern.

But what you're actually going through—that fight, the exhaustion, the way every step forward feels like it's met with a force pushing you back—that's real. And it's not weakness to feel overwhelmed by it. It's human.

Most people who speak about "life is a garden" have never had to tend one in a drought.

The Seasons of the Garden

The idea behind "Zindagi Gulzar Hai" isn't that life is always rosy. That would be a lie, and a cruel one to tell someone in the middle of their struggle.

The truth is more honest: life isn't always a garden. Sometimes it's a battlefield. Sometimes it's a desert. Sometimes it's a wasteland where nothing grows and you're just trying to survive another day.

What "Zindagi Gulzar Hai" actually means—what it *should* mean—is something different. It's the understanding that despite everything, there might still be a bloom somewhere. Even if it's small. Even if it takes forever to show. Even if you have to look for it among the rubble.

It's not about denying the struggle. It's about refusing to be defined entirely by it.

A garden doesn't bloom because conditions are perfect. It blooms because something in it—some seed, some root, some stubborn force—keeps reaching toward light even in imperfect circumstances. That's not naiveté. That's resilience. That's the real poetry.

The Bloom Isn't Guaranteed

Here's the hard part, the part that separates real understanding from motivational platitude:

The bloom isn't guaranteed.

You can fight. You can struggle. You can pour everything into growth and meaning-making. And sometimes, the bloom still doesn't come. Sometimes you tend the garden and nothing grows. Sometimes you do everything right and life still feels barren.

That's the reality many leaders face. That's the reality many people face.

But here's what matters: you fight not because life is fair. You don't persist because the universe promises you a reward. You don't keep going because you're guaranteed success.

You fight because you choose not to give in.

That choice, in itself, has meaning. Not because it guarantees an outcome. But because it defines who you are in the midst of the struggle. It's the difference between being defeated and being tested. Between giving up and still being in the fight.

When You're Knocked Down Again

And you will be knocked down again. That's not pessimism; that's pattern recognition. Anyone who's been in leadership for any length of time knows this. The struggle doesn't end. The setbacks keep coming. Just when you think you're gaining ground, something pushes you back.

The question isn't whether you'll be knocked down. The question is what happens after.

When you feel knocked down again—when exhaustion sets in, when doubt whispers, when the path seems impossible—notice this: the fact that you're still thinking about it means something. The fact that you're still feeling something about it means something. The fact that you're still trying, even in small ways, means something.

That means the story's not over.

A garden in winter looks dead. The flowers aren't blooming. The colours are muted. But beneath the frozen ground, roots are still there. Seeds are still there. The capacity to bloom is still there, even when it's invisible.

You are still there, even when the bloom isn't visible.

The Meaning in Imperfection

Leadership—real leadership—isn't about creating a perfect garden. It's not about having all the answers, making all the right calls, maintaining an image of infallibility.

Real leadership is about tending something imperfect. It's about working with people who are flawed, systems that are broken, circumstances that are unfair. It's about finding meaning not despite the imperfection, but through it.

The imperfections are where growth happens. The struggles are where character is forged. The gaps between what you hoped for and what actually happened—that's where wisdom lives.

A perfect garden would teach you nothing. A garden that survives drought, that blooms in rocky soil, that produces flowers despite neglect or harsh weather—that garden teaches you something about resilience. About adaptation. About what it means to create beauty in adverse conditions.

That's "Zindagi Gulzar Hai."

Not denial of the desert. But blooms in the desert.

The Weight Is Real, and So Is the Choice

I want to be clear about something: if you're carrying a weight that feels unbearable, that's not a sign you're weak. That's a sign you're human and you're awake to what's actually happening around you and inside you.

Overwhelm isn't failure. Exhaustion isn't a character flaw. The moments when you feel like you can't keep going—those are the moments when you're actually closest to understanding what it means to keep going anyway.

The choice isn't about feeling ready. It's about choosing to stay in the fight even when you're not ready, even when you're terrified, even when you don't believe it will work.

That choice is where the bloom comes from.

A Garden Needs Tending, Not Just Planting

Here's something leaders often miss: you can't tend a garden alone. Gardens need water, soil, sunlight—resources that come from outside yourself. They need other hands. They need community.

If you're carrying this weight—whether it's the weight of leadership, the weight of struggle, the weight of feeling like nothing is blooming—please share it with someone near and dear. Not to burden them, but to let them bear witness. Not to solve it for you, but to remind you that you're not alone in the struggle.

The bloom doesn't happen in isolation. Neither does resilience. Neither does the choice to keep fighting.

Talk to someone. Let someone see what you're carrying. That's not weakness. That's wisdom. That's the recognition that even in a garden, no plant grows entirely on its own.

Still Fighting, Still Blooming

"Zindagi Gulzar Hai" isn't about living in denial. It's not about pretending the struggle isn't real or the exhaustion isn't legitimate.

It's about understanding that even in the midst of struggle—especially in the midst of struggle—there are moments of beauty. Small blooms. Quiet victories. The moment when someone you mentored finally gets it. The project that finally works. The day when you realize you survived something you thought would break you.

It's about recognizing that you can be in a desert and still find meaning in the small oasis. You can be in a battle and still choose the moments of peace. You can be imperfect, struggling, exhausted—and still be worth fighting for. Still be blooming, in your own way, on your own timeline.

The garden doesn't bloom all at once. It blooms in seasons. It blooms despite conditions. It blooms because something in it refuses to stop reaching toward light.

That's you, too. Even when you can't see the bloom yet. Even when you're too tired to keep reaching. Even when the bloom seems impossibly far away.

You're still in the garden. You're still reaching. And the story—your story—is not over.

Part – V
Organizational Leadership & Culture

18

Governance, Risk, and Responsibility

What Governance Actually Is

Most organizations treat governance like a checkbox. Something to be reviewed once a year as part of an audit cycle. A compliance requirement. A box to tick before moving on to "real work."

But governance isn't something that happens annually. It lives in daily operations. It lives in every project decision, in every change request, in every resource strategy. It's not a document you create and file. It's a way of thinking that either permeates your organization or doesn't.

The difference between organizations that thrive and organizations that eventually collapse often comes down to this: whether governance is treated as a burden or as a safeguard.

Good governance isn't built in crisis. It's built before it. It's the infrastructure you put in place when things are relatively stable, so that when disruption comes—and it will—you're not scrambling to invent processes in the middle of chaos.

I learned this lesson repeatedly across 25 years in automotive interiors, especially working across global operations and complex supply chains. The organizations that weathered disruptions weren't the ones with the most sophisticated audit functions. They were the ones that had built governance thinking into how they operated every single day.

Risk Management: More Than an Audit Checklist

One of the most underestimated areas is risk anticipation in team deliverables. Organizations often think about risk in abstract terms—regulatory risk, market risk, strategic risk. But the risk that actually erodes performance is the risk nobody's planning for: the operational risk that emerges from daily decisions.

Take a real-world example from my experience:

When demand suddenly spikes in one location or drops in another, it throws off all resource planning. Deliverables get jeopardized. Costs inflate. Timelines slip. This isn't a rare event—it's a recurring challenge in businesses dealing with multiple markets and variable demand.

Most organizations respond reactively. Demand shifts. Chaos ensues. They scramble to reallocate resources, miss commitments, and then wonder why their costs are out of control.

A better approach: proactive risk anticipation.

To mitigate this predictable unpredictability, we maintained a strategic internal-to-external resource ratio. Not a fixed number, but a deliberate flexibility built into our resource strategy. This gave us the agility to shift resources swiftly without breaking the budget. When demand spiked somewhere, we could rebalance. When it dropped elsewhere, we could adjust. We stayed prepared, resilient, and aligned with cost optimization goals—especially during sudden business course corrections.

This isn't complicated. But it requires something most organizations lack: the foresight to plan flexibility, the courage to ask "what if," and the discipline to course-correct early.

True risk management is not reactive—it's embedded. It's woven into the way you plan, the way you resource, the way you execute. It's asking uncomfortable questions before they become crises. It's building safeguards into your processes so that when disruption comes, you're not inventing solutions in the middle of chaos.

Don't wait for a disruption to remind you of the risks you ignored. Build risk thinking into your core processes. It's the best insurance for business continuity.

Governance Frameworks and Operational Reality

As companies approach an IPO, governance suddenly becomes a value multiplier. Investors want assurance. They want to know that your organization isn't held together by heroic effort and informal relationships. They want to see frameworks. They want to see processes. They want confidence that when leadership changes, the organization doesn't collapse.

Yet many boards underestimate how operational chaos—especially across global sites—can erode investor confidence. You can have beautiful governance documents and still have a dysfunctional organization if governance isn't actually embedded in how you operate.

I've seen firsthand how governance frameworks built into the supply chain reduce compliance surprises and drive performance clarity. When you have clear decision rights, transparent escalation paths, documented risk thresholds, and mechanisms for early warning—suddenly your organization becomes more predictable. More resilient. More investable.

But here's the catch: governance frameworks only work if they're enforced consistently. And they're only enforced consistently if leadership demonstrates that governance matters more than convenience, more than protecting individuals, more than shortcuts.

The Loyalty Trap: Why Competence Must Come First

This brings us to something that erodes governance at its core: elevating loyalty over competence in appointments.

I've seen this pattern repeatedly across organizations, and it's almost always the beginning of the end for governance integrity. The individuals who get elevated aren't always incompetent—that's what makes it insidious. But the *pattern* of elevation is the problem. These are the "yes" men and women—people whose primary strength is alignment with their superior's thinking, not independent judgment or capability for the next level role.

The tragedy is what this does to the system: promotions start happening based on superior choices, not team requirements or what's better for the organization. Leaders find themselves justifying management decisions that benefit the ego and the one-track thinking of their boss, rather than advocating for what their team actually needs.

This is plainly not right. But it happens everywhere.

When you appoint people based on loyalty rather than merit, you're not just making a personnel decision. You're making a statement about your organization's values. You're saying: *Personal allegiance matters more than capability. Trust based on relationship matters more than trust based on competence. Alignment with your boss matters more than what's right for the team.*

And that statement cascades through your entire system.

What happens when loyalty replaces competence?

First, decision-making deteriorates. When people are promoted because they're aligned with their superior's thinking rather than capable of independent leadership, they often lack the judgment to make good decisions. They're not equipped to lead at the next level. So, what emerges is a pattern: "I decide, you blindly follow." Leadership becomes about authority rather than wisdom. Decisions don't get better; they get faster and more arbitrary.

Second, leaders stop advocating for their teams. When your boss expects loyalty over competence, you learn to justify their decisions rather than challenge them. You stop pushing back when a "yes" person gets promoted over a talented contributor. You stop arguing for what your team needs because the system rewards alignment, not advocacy. The leader's job—to protect and advocate for their people—gets replaced with the obligation to support whatever the boss decides.

Third, groupthink becomes entrenched. When loyalty is the primary criterion for advancement, people learn that the path to success is alignment, not challenge. People stop bringing different perspectives. Different opinions become threats rather than resources. Dissent gets silenced—not always explicitly, but through a hundred small signals that falling in line is safer than speaking up.

Fourth, organizational integrity weakens. When competence matters less than loyalty, you're no longer selecting for people who will do what's right. You're selecting for people who will do what you ask. And when those two things diverge—when doing what's right means questioning authority—the organization has lost its moral compass.

This is a classic hallmark of authoritarian-leaning leadership: valuing personal allegiance over democratic accountability. It works, briefly. It feels efficient. Decisions get made quickly. There's clarity about who's in charge. And everyone knows exactly what the promotion criteria really are—not capability, not performance, but loyalty to the person above you.

But it's fragile. It's vulnerable. And it's devastating to governance.

The Cost of Loyalty-Based Governance

Let me be specific about what are these costs:

Compliance failures emerge quietly. When people are in roles because of loyalty, they often lack the expertise to anticipate compliance risks. You don't see the problem until it's public. Until it's costly. Until it damages trust.

Innovation stalls. You need people who will challenge assumptions, who will ask "what if we did this differently?" People appointed for loyalty rarely do this. They're focused on maintaining the relationship with their sponsor, not on pushing the organization forward.

Talent leaves. The capable people in your organization—the ones who could have been developed, who could have brought different perspectives—they see that loyalty matters more than merit. So, they leave. They go to organizations where competence is valued. And you're left with loyalty and mediocrity.

Risk accelerates. When your leadership team is selected for allegiance rather than capability, they miss things. They don't ask the hard questions. They don't anticipate problems. And suddenly the risks you built governance to mitigate—they're materializing because the people responsible for mitigating them aren't capable of doing it.

Leadership Integrity and the Hard Call

Real leadership integrity shows up in moments when loyalty and competence are in conflict.

When you have someone loyal to you—someone who's been with you, who's supported you, who's shown up for you in difficult times—and you realize they're not the right fit for the role they're in or the position they're seeking. That's when integrity matters. That's when you have to choose between protecting the relationship and protecting the organization.

The easy call is loyalty. It's comfortable. It's what that person expects. It preserves the relationship in the short term. It avoids the difficult conversation and the temporary hurt.

The right call is competence. And it requires something harder than just making the decision. It requires you to sit down with that person and explain it. To make the case for why organizational need comes before loyalty. To be honest about what this means and why you're making this choice.

This is the part most leaders avoid. It's easier to make the decision quietly, or to justify it in ways that protect both the person and yourself. But that's not integrity. That's avoidance.

Real integrity means having the conversation. It means explaining your reasoning—not to convince them you're right, but to give them the respect of understanding where you stand and why. It means being clear: this isn't personal. This is professional. This is about what the organization needs, and that has to come first.

Yes, it may hurt the relationship with the individual who is loyal to you. The person might feel betrayed. They might question your loyalty to them. That's the hard part about leadership. You have to be unbiased. You have to be unemotional about the decision at hand, even when emotion is involved.

Because if you choose based on emotion—based on loyalty, based on not wanting to hurt someone, based on protecting a relationship—you've already compromised your integrity. You've already decided that the relationship matters more than the organization's health.

And that decision will be felt throughout your team. People will see that loyalty to you is more important than competence. And they'll organize their behaviour accordingly—not around doing excellent work, but around maintaining your favour.

This is never a personal choice in professional life. That's the boundary leaders must maintain. You can care about people. You can value relationships. But when a decision affects the organization, it can't be driven by personal loyalty. It has to be driven by what's right for the mission, the team, and the organization's future.

Even if it costs you personally in terms of the relationship. That's the cost of integrity.

Because here's what's at stake: your organization's governance. Your team's trust. Your investors' confidence. The careers of people who are counting on competent leadership. The morale of talented people who watch to see whether competence or loyalty determines advancement.

When you choose loyalty over competence and refuse to have the hard conversation, you're not just protecting an individual. You're undermining the entire system of governance that keeps an organization healthy. You're telling everyone in your organization that relationships trump responsibility.

But when you make the hard choice, sit down with that person, and explain it clearly—even knowing it may damage the relationship—you're modelling what integrity actually looks like. You're showing that organizational need comes first. You're saying that loyalty is valuable, but it's not more valuable than doing what's right.

That's leadership.

Building Governance That Lasts

Good governance isn't about having perfect processes. It's about having the discipline to follow the processes you've created, even—especially—when it's inconvenient.

It means:

- Appointing people based on capability first, relationship second
- Asking hard questions about risk, not once a year, but continuously
- Creating cultures where dissent is safe and different perspectives are valued
- Following your escalation procedures even when you'd prefer to handle something informally
- Making decisions based on what's right for the organization, not what's comfortable for the leader

This is unglamorous work. It doesn't make headlines. But it's what separates organizations that last from organizations that eventually collapse under the weight of poor decisions, missed risks, and eroded trust.

The Investment in Governance

As companies approach transitions—whether it's growth, leadership changes, or going public—governance becomes visibly important. Suddenly boards care. Suddenly investors ask questions. Suddenly everyone recognizes that governance matters.

But by then, if you haven't built it in already, you're starting from behind. You're trying to retrofit integrity into systems that were never designed for it.

The time to build governance is now. When things are relatively stable. When you're not in crisis. When you can invest in processes and frameworks without feeling rushed. When you can make decisions based on what's right rather than what's expedient.

Because governance built under pressure is always compromised. Governance built proactively is the only kind that actually holds.

The Leader's Choice

Every day, leaders face choices about governance:

- Whether to follow the process or take a shortcut
- Whether to appoint the loyal person or the capable one
- Whether to ask the hard question or accept the comfortable answer
- Whether to act on risk signals or hope they go away

These choices seem small in the moment. But they accumulate. They compound. They define what kind of organization you're building.

Good governance isn't about compliance. It's about integrity. It's about building an organization where people trust that decisions are made well, where risks are anticipated rather than ignored, where capability matters as much as loyalty—maybe more.

That's leadership responsibility. That's good governance. That's the foundation that lasts.

19

Captive R&D Centers in India - From Execution to Ownership

The Hard Truth

Despite being home to some of the finest engineering minds in the world, many Indian captive R&D centers continue to function as execution arms—dragged behind by their global parent organizations.

What's frustrating isn't just the underutilization of world-class talent. It's the systemic reluctance to recognize and empower it.

I've watched this pattern for years in the automotive industry. Teams that are equally—if not more—competent are assigned less strategic roles. They're limited to implementation while decision-making remains offshore. They deliver results that match or exceed global standards, yet acknowledgment is withheld. Recognition, when it comes, feels tokenistic at best.

The most disappointing part? Organizational maturity doesn't always translate to openness. In fact, it can mask a rigidity that stifles innovation and demotivates talent. Global companies with decades of experience, sophisticated processes, and impressive track records—they often remain locked in legacy mindsets about where real capability exists and where "execution" belongs.

Here's what I've come to understand: Real growth—personal, professional, and organizational—thrives on trust, transparency, and empowerment. When those are missing, so is the opportunity to build something truly transformative.

Indian talent doesn't need charity. It needs a real seat at the table.

The Gap: Execution vs. Ownership

The fundamental problem with most captive R&D centers in India isn't a shortage of capability. It's a shortage of authority.

Teams are handed specifications. They execute brilliantly. The work flows upstream to global headquarters where strategy, innovation, and decision-making happen. The center becomes a well-oiled machine for turning requirements into delivery. But it never becomes a source of strategy. It never becomes a place where "what if" questions get asked and answered. It never becomes a center of ownership.

This isn't just inefficient. It's a waste of human potential at scale. It's leaving innovation and strategic insight on the table. It's demotivating the exact people you should be developing as future leaders.

The path forward requires intentional, structural, and cultural change—from both the global parent and the Indian center. It's not a single initiative. It's a systematic reshaping of how centers are positioned, how decisions are made, and how talent is valued.

A Roadmap for Transformation

1. Shift from "Support" to "Strategic Ownership"

The foundation of everything is this: assign end-to-end ownership.

Don't just ask Indian teams to implement. Ask them to own. Give them entire modules, products, or market segments. Make them responsible for the full lifecycle—from concept through delivery through evolution. Let them experience the weight of ownership and the satisfaction of building something complete.

This also means encouraging India-first innovation. There are use cases—cost-sensitive ones, high-scale ones, ones specific to emerging markets—where Indian expertise doesn't just match global standards, it exceeds them. These shouldn't be treated as secondary markets. They should be treated as innovation laboratories. Let teams innovate for these contexts. Let them lead. Let them build products that start in India and go global.

And create product owners and architects in India, not just downstream roles. The moment an Indian engineer is sitting in the architecture conversation, the dynamic changes. They're not waiting for a specification from offshore. They're shaping it.

2. Establish Clear Pathways for Recognition and Growth

Visibility is the enemy of empowerment. If talented people are invisible to the organization, they remain undervalued. If success goes unrecognized, why should they stay?

Implement transparent career frameworks aligned with global standards. Make it clear how someone progresses. Make the criteria visible. Make it achievable.

Nominate Indian leaders for global awards, panels, and patents. Make them visible to the broader organization. Let them represent not just their center, but the organization globally.

Create cross-border peer review systems to ensure fair evaluations. The problem with center-based evaluations is they stay center-based. You need external input, global perspective, peer validation. When an Indian engineer's work is evaluated by both local and global peers, the assessment becomes richer and the visibility increases.

3. Increase Representation in Global Leadership Forums

Decisions are made in rooms you're not in. That's the core problem.

Include Indian tech leads in global architecture and strategy discussions. Not as attendees taking notes. As participants shaping the conversation.

Have India-based leaders serve on steering committees and governance boards. Let them have voting power, not just a voice.

Encourage bi-directional secondments—India to HQ and HQ to India. This is where bias breaks down. When a global leader spends time in India, sees the calibre of work, experiences the constraints and the creativity, their perspective shifts. When an Indian leader spends time at headquarters, they understand the global context and build relationships that last.

These aren't nice-to-have programs. They're structural requirements for real empowerment.

4. Invest in Executive Coaching and Exposure

Sometimes the gap isn't capability—it's exposure or communication style.

Provide executive coaching for Indian tech leaders on influencing, storytelling, and global stakeholder management. These are learnable skills, and investing in them pays dividends.

Run regular knowledge-sharing sessions between India and global teams. Not formal trainings. Real conversations where people get to know each other, where assumptions get challenged, where mutual understanding builds.

This breaks down the "us vs. them" dynamic that often exists between centers. It replaces it with "we're solving the same problem from different perspectives."

5. Redesign Organizational Structures for Autonomy

Centralized control from a global headquarters slows everything down. It also makes it clear that the center isn't trusted with real decisions.

Move toward a hub-and-spoke or multi-hub model rather than a top-down control tower. Give each hub—including India—authority over its domain.

Empower Indian centers with their own budgets, their own OKRs, and their own roadmaps. Align these with global strategy, absolutely. But don't dictate them. Let centers own their destiny.

The difference is profound. When a team sets its own roadmap, they're invested in delivering it. When a roadmap is handed down, they're executing someone else's vision.

6. Be Honest About Bias—and Tackle It Head-On

This is the part most organizations want to avoid, which is exactly why it's critical.

Acknowledge the problem: Implicit bias against offshore teams exists. It's real. It's not personal. It's systemic. Create safe spaces where employees can voice concerns without fear of retribution.

Run bias and cultural sensitivity training—not just for Indian teams, but for global teams as well. The bias isn't one-directional. Make it safe to talk about it.

Most importantly, make equity a key leadership KPI. If diversity and inclusion are just values statements on a website, nothing changes. If they're part of how leaders are evaluated, things shift quickly.

7. Create Feedback Loops That Actually Drive Change

Feedback from Indian centers often hits a wall offshore. People stop speaking up. They disengage. They leave.

Set up formal escalation and feedback mechanisms with accountability. Make it clear that when someone raises a concern, it gets heard at appropriate levels.

Track and publish actions taken on employee feedback. Transparency builds trust. When people see that their feedback led to change, they keep bringing ideas. They stay engaged.

The Vision: From Captive to Catalyst

The goal isn't to create autonomous centers that ignore global strategy. The goal is to create centers that are catalysts for innovation, value, and growth.

Indian R&D centers are not cost centers. They're not execution arms. They're value centers. They're innovation hubs. They're future-ready labs where some of the world's best engineering minds are solving complex problems.

But this potential can only be realized if we bridge the divide with mutual respect, aligned incentives, and shared purpose.

Global parents have to trust. Indian centers have to step up. And both have to commit to building something that works not because of hierarchy, but because of genuine partnership.

What This Requires

This roadmap requires courage from global leadership—the courage to distribute decision-making authority, to trust centers they don't see daily, to accept that innovation might come from places they didn't expect.

It requires courage from Indian leaders—the courage to own decisions, to push back, when necessary, to step into visibility even when you're used to working quietly.

It requires both to commit to honest conversations about bias, about power, about what real empowerment looks like.

The Competitive Advantage

Here's what most organizations miss: the companies that truly unlock the potential of their Indian R&D centers don't just get better products. They get a competitive advantage that's hard to replicate.

When you move from extraction (pulling execution out of a center) to enablement (enabling a center to create strategy and own outcomes), everything changes. Quality improves. Innovation accelerates. Retention increases. Most importantly, you develop the next generation of global leaders—leaders who understand multiple markets, who've solved complex problems, who've earned their authority through demonstrated capability, not location.

That's not a nice story about empowerment. That's a competitive moat.

The Starting Point

This transformation doesn't require a massive reorganization. It starts with a decision: to treat Indian R&D centers not as support functions, but as strategic assets.

It starts with one conversation between a global leader and an Indian team saying: "We've been treating this wrong. What would it look like if we actually empowered you? What would you build? What would you own?"

The answers to those questions will reshape how you think about innovation, about global capability, and about where real value lives.

Indian talent has been waiting for this invitation. The question is: are global organizations ready to extend it?

20

Innovation Paradox in GCCs

The Paradox

Push for innovation without exposure to free thinking. Demand breakthroughs while cutting budgets for learning. Expect creativity while enforcing hierarchy. Tell teams to experiment while making failure career-threatening. Then wonder why the innovation you're getting feels like squeezing the last remnants from a toothpaste tube.

Is this a recipe for real innovation-driven culture? No. It's a recipe for exhaustion, disengagement, and mediocrity masquerading as efficiency.

This is the GCC innovation paradox.

Global Capability Centers are built on a clear model: cost efficiency, first and foremost. Anything beyond that is a bonus. And the credit—when there is any—remains mainly with the parent or partner organization. The expectation is transparent: deliver more with less, year after year.

Into this environment, leadership injects another demand: innovation. Be creative. Think differently. Solve problems in ways we haven't thought of. Push boundaries.

But the system isn't designed for that. It's designed for the opposite.

As a leader, sometimes you really feel that the push expected—the demand for innovation within a cost-constrained, hierarchically controlled system—is not justified to the people you take for granted.

You're asking them to do the impossible. And then you're wondering why they're burning out, why the best ones are leaving, why what you're calling "innovation" feels forced and hollow.

What Are We Actually Asking For?

Before we talk about solutions, we need to be honest about what's actually happening.

When a GCC is asked to innovate while remaining cost-optimized, what are we really asking for? Recognition? Incentives? Or just plain survival?

The answer is usually survival. The parent organization wants efficiency. They also want innovation, but only if it doesn't compromise efficiency. That's the contradiction baked into the system.

And the people in the center feel it viscerally. They're not being asked to innovate because the organization believes in their potential. They're being asked to innovate because the organization needs competitive advantage—and they need to deliver it without any additional resources. The expectation is that innovation comes from working harder, thinking smarter, sacrificing more.

This is a broken contract. And everyone knows it's broken. But it persists because the alternative—fundamentally reshaping how GCCs work—requires courage from both the parent organization and local leadership.

So, what you get is people coping. People performing. People extracting every ounce of effort from themselves and their teams while knowing it's not sustainable and not what real innovation looks like.

That's not a culture of innovation. That's a culture of survival dressed up in innovation language.

The Real Obstacles to Innovation in GCCs

Cost constraints don't just limit budgets—they limit mindsets. When every rupee is accounted for, when every hour must be billable, there's no room for experimentation. There's no room for the 80% of ideas that won't work. There's no room for learning that doesn't immediately translate to revenue. People stop proposing ideas. They stop thinking sideways. They think in straight lines: minimum input, maximum output.

Hierarchy doesn't just slow decisions—it kills permission. When the organizational structure is rigid, when authority is concentrated, when ideas have to flow up multiple levels before they get approved, something happens: people stop bringing ideas. Not because they don't have them, but because the friction is too high. By the time an idea navigates the approval chain, the moment has passed. The person who had the idea has moved on to something else. And the organization loses the energy and insight that real innovation needs.

Lack of psychological safety doesn't just create fear—it creates compliance. When failure is career-threatening, when mistakes get punished, when the environment signals "don't take risks," people optimize for survival, not innovation. They do what's asked. They deliver what's expected. They don't experiment. They don't push boundaries. They don't bring their full creativity to the table.

Taken together, these three things—cost constraints, hierarchy, and lack of psychological safety—don't just make innovation harder. They make it nearly impossible.

And yet the organization keeps pushing for it. Keeps wondering why it's not happening. Keeps blaming the people instead of examining the system.

What Leaders Must Do: A Pragmatic Path

If you're a leader in a GCC facing this paradox, you have a choice. You can enable the broken system. Or you can transform it from within.

Transforming it doesn't mean revolution. It means strategy. It means understanding what you can change and what you need to navigate. It means building capability and capital to create space for real innovation.

1. Insulate Your Team from Hierarchical Pressures—First and Foremost

This is your primary responsibility as a leader. Not to eliminate hierarchy—you can't. But to create a buffer between your team and unnecessary pressure from above.

This means:

- Being the shock absorber for unrealistic expectations
- Fighting for your team's autonomy in how they approach problems
- Creating psychological safety within your sphere of influence
- Protecting people who take smart risks from political consequences
- Building trust so people feel safe bringing half-formed ideas, experiments, and even failures to you

You can't change the system from above. But you can change the environment immediately around your team. You can make your team a place where thinking differently isn't career-threatening.

2. Fight for Small Wins: Learning, Time, Autonomy

You don't need massive change to create space for innovation. You need small, deliberate moves that accumulate over time.

Budget for learning and experimentation. Even 2–5% of time or resources dedicated to learning, experimentation, or skill development can pay off. This isn't extravagant. This isn't asking for moonshot budgets. This is asking for the resources to keep people's skills current, to let them explore emerging technologies, to spend time on problems that don't have immediate billable value.

Make the case with data: What skills are becoming critical? What capabilities will we need in two years? What emerging technologies are our competitors exploring? Reframe learning not as a cost, but as staying competitive.

Carve out time for autonomy. Even within a constrained system, you can create space where people aren't being microscoped. Where they can spend a few hours exploring an idea without needing approval. Where they can fail on a small scale without consequences.

Create a wedge for different ways of working. Set up internal innovation sprints, labs, or hackathons without external pressure. These aren't grand initiatives. They're structured spaces where people can think differently without threatening the core delivery. They build momentum. They show what's possible. They keep creative people engaged.

3. Play the Long Game

Yes, sometimes it is about survival. The GCC has to deliver what the parent organization expects. You can't ignore that. But survival doesn't mean you can't simultaneously work toward transformation.

Push back diplomatically when goals are unrealistic. Don't just accept impossible mandates. Engage in real conversation about what's achievable, what the trade-offs are, what gets sacrificed if you push too hard. Most leaders overestimate how much you can say "no" if you frame it in terms of what matters to the organization.

Advocate for structural change with data. Collect evidence. Show what happens when you invest in learning—retention improves, quality improves, people stay engaged. Show what happens when you give teams autonomy—they solve problems faster, they take ownership. Make the case not as an emotional plea, but as a business argument.

Build a leadership culture beneath you that believes in more than cost savings. This is the long game. Develop leaders who understand that culture, retention, quality, and innovation matter. Leaders who can hold two truths simultaneously: "We have to deliver on cost" and "We also have to invest in people and capability." Leaders who can navigate the system without being consumed by it.

4. Reflect on Your Role in the System

This is the hardest part. And it's necessary.

Am I enabling a broken system or transforming it from within? Be honest with yourself. Are you accepting things as they are because it's easier? Or are you actively working toward change? There's a difference between pragmatism and complicity.

Are my people growing under my leadership—or just coping? This is your real measure. Not the cost efficiency you deliver. Not the projects you complete. But whether the people under your leadership are developing, learning, becoming more capable and engaged. If they're just surviving, something needs to change.

Do I have the political capital to negotiate change—or do I need to build it first? Sometimes you don't have the standing yet to push for major change. Then your job is to build it. Deliver results. Build trust. Create credibility. Then use that capital to negotiate for something different.

What Real Innovation Actually Requires

Innovation doesn't happen in constrained environments. It happens when people have permission to think differently, resources to explore, time to experiment, and psychological safety to fail.

You can't give all of these things. But you can give some. And you can fight for the conditions that would make innovation possible rather than accepting that it's impossible.

You can create pockets of possibility. You can protect people from the full weight of the hierarchy. You can invest in learning even when it seems like a luxury. You can create space where experimentation is safe.

You can't transform the entire GCC model from your position. But you can transform how your team experiences working within it. You can create an environment where people aren't just coping—they're growing. You can plant the seeds of a different culture.

And sometimes, that's where real change begins.

The Questions That Matter

At the end of every week, ask yourself:

Did I protect my people from unnecessary pressure? Did I buffer them from chaos coming from above? Did I fight for their autonomy?

Did I create any small space for learning or experimentation? Even tiny pockets where people could think differently without fear?

Did I make a case for why the current model is limiting? Did I gather data, build arguments, advocate for change?

Am I building leadership beneath me that understands this? Am I developing the next generation of leaders who won't accept the broken system as inevitable?

Are my people growing—or are they just getting tired?

These questions define your leadership in a GCC environment. Not whether you hit cost targets. Not whether you delivered projects. But whether you're complicit in a broken system or actively working to transform it from within.

The Bigger Picture

This matters beyond your team. How GCC leaders handle the innovation paradox shapes whether these centers become true innovation hubs or remain extractive cost centers. It shapes whether the best talent stays or leaves. It shapes whether the organizations you work for stay competitive or slowly fall behind.

The paradox exists because of how GCCs were originally conceived—as cost optimization centers. But the world has changed. Competition is different. The future belongs to organizations that can innovate globally, not just execute globally.

That requires GCCs to actually innovate. Which requires leaders who are willing to protect, fight for, and build the conditions that make innovation possible.

Even when the system wasn't designed for it. Especially then.

21

The Efficiency Illusion

The Spectacle

There's a recurring spectacle in most large organizations that's both familiar and frustrating. I call it "The Efficiency Illusion."

It looks like progress. It feels like action. It even sounds strategic. But in reality, it often amounts to little more than an orchestrated echo chamber dressed up as transformation.

I've witnessed this pattern time and again, especially during Year-on-Year strategy planning or efficiency alignment meetings. The ritual is so consistent you could set a watch by it. And the tragedy is that everyone involved—from the senior leaders designing the process to the frontline managers participating in it—knows, at some level, that the process is hollow. Yet it persists. Because the alternative—genuine uncertainty, real experimentation, actual risk of failure—feels more dangerous than maintaining the comfortable illusion.

The Scripted Efficiency Ritual

The pattern unfolds like clockwork.

Step 1: We kick things off with energy.

Grand speeches. A rallying call for transformation. A clear message: this time will be different. We need to think bigger. We need to be braver. We need to challenge the status quo.

Then we divide teams into "working groups," each with a charter to explore paths to greater efficiency. Everyone feels the electricity. This is going to be it. This is going to move the needle.

Step 2: The working groups get to work.

Discussions ensue. Whiteboards fill up. PowerPoints multiply. But notice what's actually happening: the discussions move along well-trodden paths. "Standardize processes." "Commonize platforms." "Automate operations." "Leverage best practices." "Consolidate functions."

All of which, mind you, are safe bets. Comfortable clichés. They're not wrong, exactly. But they're not novel either. They're the ideas that have been recycled in a hundred efficiency initiatives before this one. Everyone knows what "automation" looks like. Everyone can talk about "best practices." There's no intellectual risk. There's no real exposure.

The thinking is safe. The recommendations are predictable. The path is well-worn.

Step 3: Each group presents their findings.

The room is arranged for theatre. Production value is high. Charts are polished. Narratives are tight. Everyone presents essentially the same ideas in slightly different language because they're all drawing from the same conceptual well.

Everyone claps. The energy is kept high. Optics are great. Boxes are ticked.

Step 4: The same ideas—echoed across groups—are handed over to a "core team" for deeper evaluation and potential implementation.

This team is supposed to be the guardians of rigor. The ones who push back. The ones who ask hard questions.

But they rarely do. Because they too are part of the same cultural current. They operate within the same constraints. They face the same pressures. They've sat through the same speeches about courage while operating within the same risk-averse systems. So, what happens? The ideas that came out of the working groups get marginally refined, ranked by what seems most achievable, and handed over to be "implemented."

The session ends with a sense of satisfaction. We did it. We explored. We challenged ourselves. Progress was made.

The Outcome: A Mirage of Progress

But here's what actually happened:

No real experimentation. No one was genuinely encouraged to try something that might fail. No courage to question the status quo in any way that matters. No tolerance for micro-innovations—the small, scrappy experiments that might lead somewhere unexpected. No space for messy, real-world examples where things didn't work, because those don't fit the narrative of progress.

Most efficiency efforts end up chasing only large percentage cost reductions. Thirty percent here, twenty percent there. Those make headlines. Those impress investors. Those justify the effort.

Meanwhile, the smaller, incremental gains—the kind that could collectively drive long-term culture and performance—are considered "not worth the effort." They don't move the needle visibly. They don't generate a compelling story. So, they're ignored.

And so, the organization ends up with an efficiency roadmap that looks impressive on paper but fails to generate the kind of sustained transformation that actually changes how work happens.

Where Is the Curiosity?

Here's what's missing from the entire ritual: curiosity.

True efficiency isn't just about how much cost you can slash. It's about how well you can understand your processes. It's about learning from the field—from the people actually doing the work. It's about trying new things with discipline and urgency, and learning from what works and what doesn't.

But that requires a fundamentally different culture. It requires curiosity. It requires courage. It requires something most large organizations have systematically squeezed out of their systems.

Think about what a genuinely efficient organization would ask:

How many frontline managers were encouraged to try something new and reflect on the outcome? Not how many participated in the working groups. How many actually went back to their teams and said, "Let's experiment. Let's try a different way of organizing this work. Let's see what happens."

How many grassroots experiments were documented and built upon? Not how many efficiency initiatives were launched top-down. How many good ideas percolated up from the frontlines and got real support?

How often do we reward incremental, local optimizations rather than waiting for a big bang? Can a team get credit for a five percent improvement in their process, or do we only celebrate the transformation initiatives?

The honest answers? Almost never. Almost never. Almost never.

Our systems are so wired to seek "big efficiency wins" that we ignore the small, scrappy wins that lead to real cultural shift. We're so focused on the narrative of transformation that we miss the actual transformation happening in small pockets, waiting to be noticed and amplified.

Efficiency Must Be Learned, Not Just Managed

Here's the distinction that matters: Efficiency isn't a project. It's a mindset.

A project has a start date and an end date. You execute. You declare success. You move on.

A mindset is something you build into how people think and work every single day. It requires iterative action. It requires feedback loops. It requires trust in your teams to experiment without fear. It requires the understanding that not every solution will work—and that's the point. That's how you learn.

But most organizations treat efficiency like a project. They launch initiatives. They set targets. They monitor progress. And when the initiative ends, so does the focus on efficiency. Back to business as usual.

The illusion is believing that well-run meetings, catchy phrases, and action plan equal impact. The reality is that without execution at the edge—without frontline teams trying things and learning—and without a culture of continuous learning that rewards experimentation, you're just turning the same wheel, only with better slides.

You're creating an echo chamber where everyone confirms what everyone already knows, packages it nicely, and calls it transformation.

The Real Cost of the Illusion

Let me be specific about what these costs organizations:

Time: Enormous amounts of productive time get consumed in planning meetings, working group sessions, presentation prep, and review cycles. People who could be doing actual work are sitting in rooms talking about doing work.

Energy: The initial energy of "this time will be different" gets dissipated in the ritual. By the time recommendations come out, the momentum is gone. People are tired. Cynicism sets in.

Talent: Your best people—the ones with genuine curiosity about how to do things better—see through the illusion quickly. They see the ritual for what it is: a performance. And they leave. They go to organizations where their ideas might actually be tried. Where experimentation is safe. Where efficiency is a mindset, not a project.

Learning: The organization doesn't actually learn. Each efficiency initiative reinvents the wheel because the learning from the last initiative didn't stick. There's no accumulation of knowledge. There's just repetition.

Culture: Most insidiously, the efficiency illusion teaches people that the real work isn't execution—it's looking like you're executing. It teaches people to optimize for appearances. To play it safe. To echo back what leadership wants to hear.

That's the real cost. A culture where people are afraid to experiment, where thinking differently is risky, where safety and conformity are rewarded over curiosity and courage.

Breaking the Illusion Requires Honesty

If you're a leader, start here. Ask yourself these questions. And be honest:

When did I last encourage a team to trial something experimental? Not talk about it. Actually, try it. With real resources. With real support. With real permission to fail.

How many efficiency initiatives came from the ground up, not top down? Are frontline teams bringing ideas to you, or are you handing down solutions?

Do I reward people for playing it safe or for trying something smart—even if it fails? What does your organization actually value? What gets celebrated? What gets punished?

Am I part of maintaining the efficiency illusion, or am I working to break it? This is the hard one. Because breaking it requires you to tolerate more ambiguity, more failure, more messiness in the short term. It requires you to have fewer grand initiatives and more small experiments. It requires you to admit that not everything can be planned and controlled.

What Real Efficiency Looks Like

Real efficiency isn't smooth. It's not high-production-value presentations and well-organized working groups. It's messy. It's experimental. It's full of small failures and small wins that accumulate over time.

Real efficiency looks like:

Frontline experimentation. A team tries a new way of organizing their work. It works. They document it. Other teams learn from it. It spreads. No grand initiative. No executive sponsor. Just learning and adaptation.

Psychological safety. People bring ideas without fear that a bad idea will tank their career. They try things. Some work. Some don't. And they talk about both openly.

Distributed decision-making. Authority to experiment exists at the edge, not just at the center. Teams can try things without waiting for approval from three levels up.

Continuous feedback loops. Not annual reviews of efficiency. Weekly or monthly reflection on what's working, what's not, what we're learning.

Reward structures that align with reality. People are rewarded for trying smart things, not for hitting predetermined targets. For learning, not for playing it safe.

This doesn't sound as impressive as a grand transformation initiative. It won't fill a PowerPoint. It won't generate a compelling narrative for investors.

But it actually works. It actually changes how organizations operate. It actually drives sustained improvement.

The Paradox

Here's the paradox at the heart of all this: organizations that are truly efficient in the long term are inefficient in the short term. They waste time experimenting. They tolerate failure. They move slowly on some things because they're learning. They're not optimized. Not yet.

But because they're learning, because they're experimenting, because they're building a culture where curiosity is safe, they get better over time. Continuously. Sustainably.

Organizations that chase the appearance of efficiency—that maintain the ritual, that avoid genuine experimentation, that reward conformity—they might look efficient in the short term. All that activity. All those initiatives. Looks productive.

But they're not getting better. They're just rearranging the same pieces.

And eventually, they lose to organizations that had the courage to be inefficient in the short term.

For Leaders: The Uncomfortable Choice

You have a choice about what kind of leader you want to be in the face of this illusion.

You can participate in it. Show up to the meetings. Nod along. Present the polished findings. Keep the ritual alive. It's comfortable. It's what's expected. It works, in the short term.

Or you can work to break it. Encourage your team to bring real ideas, not safe ones. Give them permission to experiment. Document what you learn. Spread it. Build a culture where efficiency is something people do, not something they talk about in meetings.

The second path is harder. It requires you to push back sometimes. To ask uncomfortable questions. To tolerate more ambiguity and failure in your sphere of influence.

But the payoff is real: a team that actually gets better over time. People who stay because they're doing meaningful work. Results that compound because they're built on genuine learning, not just activity.

The Question That Matters Most

In the long run, it's not the illusion of efficiency that wins. It's the courage to be inefficient in the short term to get truly effective in the long term.

The question is: are you willing to have that courage? Are you willing to break the ritual? Are you willing to lead differently, even when it looks less impressive than the alternative?

Because that's where real transformation happens. Not in the meetings. Not in the working groups. Not in the polished presentations.

It happens when a leader says: we're going to do things differently. We're going to experiment. We're going to learn. We're going to be messy and uncertain for a while. But we're going to get better.

And then actually does it.

Part – VI

Personal Leadership Lessons

22

The Leader's Mirror - Building Psychological Safety in Teams

Part 1: Creating a Culture Where Silence Isn't Mistaken for Alignment

The Cost of Silence

I've never been comfortable with the kind of culture where silence is mistaken for alignment. The moment you start reading lack of pushback as agreement, you've become blind. People have learned to keep their heads down. To not rock the boat. To let bad decisions proceed unchallenged because speaking up feels too risky.

And you think you're leading. But you're flying blind. No matter how smart the strategy looks on paper, no matter how carefully you've thought through the decision, if your team isn't willing to tell you what they actually think, you're missing critical information.

Early in my career, I recognized this. I saw teams where people nodded in meetings and complained in hallways. Where the real conversations happened after the official conversation ended. Where dissent was treated as disloyalty. And I understood: that's not a high-performing team. That's a team that's learned to hide.

I made a choice then: I wasn't going to build that kind of culture.

But recognizing the problem and changing the behaviour are two very different battles.

The Work It Takes

Encouraging a true speak-up culture takes more than intent. It requires consistency, humility, and a lot of patience. A lot of patience.

I've had to push against ingrained habits—both my own and my teams.' I've had to reassure people repeatedly that dissent isn't disloyalty. That bringing a different perspective isn't a threat to my authority. That if you see a problem, your job is to say so.

I've had to model what it looks like to welcome hard truths without defensiveness. To ask genuine questions about why someone disagrees, not to poke holes in their argument. To say, "I hadn't thought of it that way—thank you for bringing that."

And even with all that, it takes time. People have been conditioned by other leaders, other organizations, other experiences to keep quiet. You can't undo that in a short period of time. You undo it by consistency. By proving, again and again, that it's actually safe.

The Mirror Test

The biggest lesson I've learned is this: people watch what you do, not what you say.

You can make all the speeches you want about valuing a different perspective. You can say all the right things about welcome feedback. But the moment someone brings up a hard truth and you respond defensively, you've undone months of work. The moment you shoot down an idea that challenges your thinking, people see it. And they make a calculation: is it really safe to speak up, or was that just talk?

Every single time someone brings up a hard truth and sees it met with curiosity instead of consequence, the culture shifts. Slowly. Meaningfully. But it shifts.

And every time someone speaks up and gets punished—even subtly, even unintentionally—the culture shifts back.

That's why consistency matters. Why your response in the moment matters. Why your humility matters.

The Question That Keeps Me Honest

I keep one question close: **What critical information might your team be afraid to tell you right now?**

I don't ask this because I assume fear is present. I ask it because I know safety is something you have to earn every single day. It's not a destination you reach. It's a commitment you renew constantly.

When I ask that question honestly, it forces me to think about what messages I might be sending unintentionally. What topics feel off-limits? What kinds of ideas get shut down quickly? Where am I being defensive without realizing it?

Sometimes the answer is uncomfortable. Sometimes I realize I've created barriers to candour without intending to. And that's when the real work happens—acknowledging it, adjusting, and proving through my behaviour that it's actually safe now.

The Three-Word Test

If your team can hear those three words from you and believe them, you've built something real:

"You are right."

Not "you have a point." Not "I hadn't thought of that." But the ability to genuinely say "you are right, and I was wrong."

Can your team hear that from you? Or does the hierarchy make that impossible? Does your ego make that impossible?

Because if people never hear those words, they stop bringing hard truths. They stop challenging. They stop thinking that their perspective matters. And you go back to flying blind.

Part 2: Insecurity Sounds like Control. Confidence Sounds Like Trust.

The Subtle Damage of Insecurity

One of the most subtle—but damaging—traits I've observed in leadership is insecurity. And it's quite common.

It doesn't always show up as obvious weakness. That would be easier to identify. Instead, it shows up as something that looks like strength: the need to have the last word. The compulsion to reframe every idea as your own. The quick dismissal of dissent as disloyalty. The careful management of credit so that your contributions are always visible and others are diminished.

I've seen this behaviour slow down decisions. A leader needs to be consulted on everything because nothing can happen without their approval. I've seen it suppress innovation. Ideas don't surface because people know the leader will claim them or kill them. I've seen it quietly erode trust. People stop believing the leader is actually invested in the best outcome—they're invested in looking good.

The tragic irony? People can feel it. They sense the insecurity beneath the controlling behaviour. And it makes them less likely to trust, not more. Less likely to follow, not more. Less likely to bring their best thinking, not more.

What Confident Leadership Actually Looks Like

The most effective leaders I've worked with aren't afraid to say, "That's a better idea than mine—let's go with it."

They say it without resentment. Without caveats. Without later claiming that they suggested it first. They say it and actually mean it.

Do they have their own ideas? Yes, of course. Strong ideas. They put those ideas on the table. They argue for them. They make a case.

But when a better idea surfaces—even if it comes from someone they supervise, even if it contradicts their initial thinking—they recognize it. They acknowledge it. They move toward it.

That's not weakness. That's strength. That's a leader secure enough in their value that they don't need to be right about every decision.

The Courage It Takes

What I've noticed is that people often stay silent not because they're afraid of consequences, but because they're afraid of their boss's ego.

They think: "My manager will take this badly. She needs to feel like the smartest person in the room. If I bring this idea, she'll either claim it as her own or find a way to shoot it down."

And they're probably right. Not because the manager is a bad person. But because somewhere along the way, that manager confused leadership with being in control. With having all the answers. With never being wrong.

So, people make a calculation. It's the one you know well if you've worked in hierarchical organizations: *Mera boss kaise lega?* How will my boss take this?

And if the answer is "probably not well," they stay silent.

The most toxic environments aren't the ones where people are openly bullied. They're the ones where people self-censor because the leader's insecurity makes real conversation feel unsafe.

The Two Choices

Here's what I've learned: in most situations, you have two choices.

You have the choice that looks good in the moment—the one that protects your ego, maintains your image, keeps you in control.

And you have the choice that actually builds something—the one that might make you look uncertain, might involve admitting you didn't think of something, might mean letting someone else's idea take center stage.

Most people choose the first one. Not because they're consciously trying to be destructive. But because they're intimidated. Because they're not sure their value survives not being right about everything. Because somewhere they learned that leaders need to have all the answers.

The hard choice is the second one. It takes courage. It takes genuine security in your value. It takes trusting that your leadership isn't defined by being right about every decision—it's defined by creating an environment where the right decisions surface.

What Confidence Actually Sounds Like

Confidence listens. Insecurity talks.

An insecure leader talks because silence feels like vulnerability. They fill every space. They explain. They justify. They make sure their thinking is visible. Because if it's not visible, they worry people will think they don't have any.

A confident leader listens. They ask questions. They sit with the discomfort of not knowing. They make space for others to think. They don't need to fill every silence with their own ideas.

This isn't about being passive. A confident leader still brings their perspective. Still makes decisions. Still provides direction.

But they do it from a place of security, not a place of fear. They're not protecting their image. They're protecting the quality of the thinking and the safety of the people doing it.

The Real Question

If you're in a position of influence, the question you need to ask yourself isn't: "Did I get my way?"

The real question is: "Did we get to the right outcome—and did my team feel safe helping us get there?"

If you got your way but people feel smaller, less heard, less valued—you didn't actually win. You just maintained control.

But if the outcome is solid and your team feels like their thinking mattered, like they could bring their real perspective, like they were heard even when they disagreed—then you've done something real. You've built something that lasts.

The Practice

Building this kind of culture—where people feel safe speaking up and where confidence sounds like trust, not control—requires daily practice.

It means:

- Explicitly inviting dissent, not just saying you welcome it
- Asking "what am I missing?" and actually listening to the answer
- Acknowledging when someone's idea is better than yours
- Protecting people who bring hard truths
- Responding to disagreement with curiosity, not defensiveness
- Making it clear that loyalty doesn't mean agreement

It means being willing to look uncertain sometimes. To admit you don't know. To let the best idea win, regardless of where it came from.

It means understanding that your role isn't to be the smartest person in the room. It's to create an environment where smart thinking can happen. Where people feel safe thinking. Where dissent is seen as contribution, not threat.

The Payoff

Teams that speak up move faster. They catch problems earlier. They innovate because people aren't afraid to suggest something unconventional. They retain talent because people want to work somewhere their thinking matters.

And leaders who've built this kind of culture? They're not stressed about being wrong. They're not burning energy managing their image. They're free to actually lead—to make decisions with better information, to develop people, to build something that lasts.

The choice between insecurity and confidence, between control and trust, isn't really about your personality or your style. It's about what you're willing to sacrifice to stay in power versus what you're willing to risk to build something real.

The Moment That Matters Most

The moment that defines your leadership—the one your team remembers and talks about—is often not the brilliant decision you made or the vision you articulated.

It's the moment when someone brought you a hard truth. When they said something that challenged you. When they disagreed.

And you heard them. You really heard them. Not to find the flaw in their thinking, but to understand it. You considered it. You let it change your mind.

That moment, more than any speech, tells your team that it's actually safe to speak up. That dissent isn't disloyalty. That their thinking matters.

And that's when the real culture shift happens. That's when people start bringing their full selves to work. That's when the best ideas surface.

That's when you stop flying blind and actually start leading

23

Captain on the Bridge

Why Kirk Matters

There's a reason Captain James T. Kirk has remained an icon for nearly sixty years. It's not the dramatic pauses or the torn uniform shirts. It's not even the one-liners or the seat-of-the-pants heroics.

It's because he understood something fundamental about leadership that most organizations have forgotten: the captain belongs on the bridge.

Not in a conference room reviewing data. Not in an office protected by layers of bureaucracy. On the bridge. Where decisions happen. Where information flows. Where accountability is visible. Where the crew can see you making the call.

Kirk's Enterprise operated as a tight, high-performing team in an environment of constant uncertainty. They faced the unknown. They made decisions with incomplete information. They succeeded not because they had all the answers, but because the captain had built a culture of trust, bold thinking, and shared purpose that allowed excellence to emerge even in chaos.

There are leadership lessons in that—real, applicable lessons—that I've tried to follow throughout my career.

Lesson 1: Trust Your Crew

Kirk never pretended to be the smartest person on the Enterprise. That would have been absurd. Spock was the scientist. McCoy was the physician. Scotty understood the ship's systems like no one else. Uhura was the communications expert.

What Kirk did was delegate effectively. More than that, he actually trusted the people he delegated to.

This is rarer than it should be. Many leaders delegate tasks. Few actually delegate authority and trust. They want to control outcomes. They want visibility into every decision. They want the final say.

Kirk didn't work that way. He gave Spock a mission, then trusted Spock to execute it. He asked McCoy for a medical opinion, then actually listened—even when it contradicted what he wanted to do. He told Scotty to get the engines online and trusted that Scotty would do it, even if Scotty said it was impossible.

And here's the thing: because Kirk trusted them, they trusted him. They showed up with their best thinking. They took ownership of their work. They weren't executing someone else's vision—they were contributing to something shared.

That's the dynamic every leader should be building. Not a hierarchy of command, but a network of trust where people feel genuinely empowered to bring their capability to the mission.

Great leadership is about building a team you can trust. And then actually trusting them.

Lesson 2: Question the Rules

There's a famous scenario from Star Trek lore—the Kobayashi Maru test. A no-win scenario. A test designed to be unwinnable. A way to see how someone responds to an impossible situation.

Kirk's answer? He didn't accept the premise. He rewrote the test. He challenged the fundamental assumption that it had to be unwinnable. He broke the rules to win.

That's not recklessness. That's leadership. That's the understanding that sometimes the rules themselves are the problem. Sometimes to survive, to progress, to solve the real problem—you have to challenge the premise you've been given.

I've worked in organizations where this was the cardinal sin. Where questioning the rules was seen as disloyalty. Where the mandate was "these are the constraints, work within them" rather than "these are the constraints—are they actually the real constraints?"

Kirk showed something different. He didn't break rules arbitrarily. He didn't dismiss structure or governance. But when the rules led to the wrong outcome—when following them meant failure—he was willing to challenge the premise.

In a world of constant change, this is essential. The rules you made five years ago might be constraints today. The assumptions that made sense when the environment was stable might be wrong now. The organization that can question its own premises is the organization that can adapt.

That requires leaders brave enough to ask: Is this rule actually necessary? Is this assumption actually true? Are we solving the real problem, or the problem we've always assumed exists?

Lesson 3: Lead from the Front

Kirk never sent his crew on a mission he wasn't willing to go on himself. He went on the away missions. He faced the danger. He took the risk first.

This is what "captain on the bridge" actually means. It means visibility. It means accountability. It means you're not in a safe room sending others into uncertain situations.

I've seen so much leadership-by-distance in modern organizations. Leaders who stay in their offices while frontline teams carry the weight. Leaders who make decisions that affect others without experiencing the consequences themselves. Leaders who demand boldness from their teams while playing it safe personally.

That's not leadership. That's management from a distance.

Real leadership means showing up where it matters. Being visible when things are difficult. Taking the risk yourself first, so your team knows you're not asking them to do something you won't do. Standing with them when outcomes are uncertain.

This doesn't mean recklessness. It means presence. It means accountability. It means your team can see you making the hard call, not just demanding they execute it.

When people see their leader willing to take risk, willing to be on the front lines, willing to be accountable publicly—they follow differently. They trust differently. They take ownership differently.

Lesson 4: Stay Curious and Open-Minded

Kirk's mission was exploration. "To boldly go where no one has gone before." But exploration isn't just about discovering new places. It's about maintaining a posture of curiosity. An openness to what you don't know. A willingness to be wrong.

Kirk encountered alien civilizations with values different from his own. He met beings with different ways of thinking. He faced situations that challenged his assumptions about how the universe worked.

And he stayed curious. He asked questions. He listened. He adjusted his thinking based on new information.

This is a leadership quality that's increasingly rare. Many leaders think they've figured it out. They have a framework, a philosophy, an approach—and they apply it consistently, regardless of what the situation requires. They're efficient in their thinking. Also wrong, frequently.

Kirk understood that leadership in uncertain environments requires staying open. Not changing direction constantly—that's not confidence, that's flailing. But genuinely maintaining curiosity about what you don't know. Asking questions. Learning from your team. Adjusting when new information emerges.

In a world of rapid change, this openness isn't a luxury. It's essential. The leader who thinks they understand the full situation is the leader who misses what's changing around them.

Lesson 5: Own Your Mistakes

This might be the rarest quality in leadership today. Kirk made decisions that didn't work out. Crew members got hurt. Missions failed. And he owned it.

Not by deflecting. Not by explaining why it wasn't his fault. Not by blaming circumstances. By saying: "I made that call. Here's what I learned. Here's how we move forward."

There's a vulnerability in that. A willingness to be seen as fallible. A recognition that leadership isn't about being infallible—it's about being accountable.

Most organizations have created systems where mistakes get hidden. Where blame gets distributed. Where no one is actually responsible. Leaders protect themselves. Middle managers protect their teams. Individual contributors stay quiet.

And the organization doesn't learn. The same mistakes repeat. People become cynical because they see mistakes swept under the rug while individuals are thrown under the bus.

Kirk modelled something different. He owned his decisions. He acknowledged when things didn't go as planned. He didn't ask his crew to sacrifice for a leader who wouldn't admit error.

That's rare. And it's powerful.

Lesson 6: Bold—Risk Is Our Business

There's a line Kirk used: "Risk is our business."

It wasn't said with bravado. It was said with clarity. The Enterprise was sent into unknown space to encounter unknown threats. Risk wasn't incidental to the mission—it was central to it. You don't explore safely. You don't discover while staying in familiar territory. You don't progress without taking calculated risks.

And Kirk's point was: if you can't accept risk, you can't do this mission. You can't explore. You can't grow. You can't lead.

I think about this a lot in organizations. There's often a culture of risk aversion. Decisions get made by committee to distribute responsibility. Innovation gets suppressed because it might fail. Bold moves don't happen because the safe move is easier to justify.

But what that means is: you don't actually progress. You optimize what you already have. You become incrementally more efficient at doing what's been done before. You don't lead into the future—you manage the past.

Kirk understood that progress requires calculated risk. Not recklessness. Not gambling. But the willingness to do something new, knowing it might not work, because the alternative—doing nothing differently—is worse.

The question for leaders isn't "Can I eliminate risk?" The question is "Can I take calculated risk confidently?"

The Bridge as a Metaphor

When I think about "the captain on the bridge," I'm not just thinking about Kirk's fictional starship. I'm thinking about what that image represents.

The bridge is where decisions get made. It's where information flows. It's where the captain has visibility and accountability. It's where the crew can see the captain making the call, not just demanding execution from a distance.

It's visible. It's real. It's accountable.

Too many modern leaders have abandoned the bridge. They're in their offices. They're in their emails. They're one or two layers removed from where actual work happens. They make decisions in private and announce them afterward. They're safe from visibility and accountability.

That's not leadership. That's management by distance.

Being the captain on the bridge means:

- You're visible when it matters
- You make decisions with your team watching
- You're accountable for those decisions publicly
- You're willing to take risk yourself first
- You're present in moments of uncertainty

It means your team doesn't have to guess what you think. They don't have to play politics to understand your priorities. They can see how you make decisions. They can watch how you respond to uncertainty, to failure, to challenge.

That visibility builds trust. That accountability builds credibility. That presence builds culture.

The Courage It Takes

Everything I've described—trusting your crew, questioning rules, leading from the front, staying curious, owning mistakes, embracing calculated risk—requires courage.

It requires courage to trust people with real authority and not micromanage. To question rules, you've built. To be visible and accountable. To stay open to being wrong. To admit mistakes. To take risks.

Most of these things feel riskier than staying safe. And in the short term, they might be. You might get hurt. You might look bad. You might face challenge.

But in the long term, these are the things that build organizations that actually work. That develop talent. That innovate. That endure.

Kirk had that courage. He trusted his crew even when they challenged him. He questioned premises that others accepted. He led from the front even when it was dangerous. He stayed curious even when he could have relied on experience. He owned his mistakes even when blame could have gone elsewhere. He embraced risk even when safety was an option.

And the Enterprise became the most storied ship in Starfleet not because it was the biggest or the strongest, but because the captain and crew worked together as a high-performing team focused on a shared mission.

The Question for Leaders

If you're leading, ask yourself:

- **Am I actually on the bridge?** Or am I staying safe in the background while expecting my team to take the risk?
- **Do I trust my crew?** Not in theory, but in practice? Do I actually delegate authority, or just tasks?
- **Have I questioned my own premises lately?** Or am I applying yesterday's rules to today's problems?
- **Am I leading from the front?** Or am I asking others to do what I won't do?
- **Do I stay curious?** Or have I stopped learning?
- **Can I own my mistakes?** Or do I find ways to distribute blame?
- **Am I willing to take calculated risks?** Or have I optimized for safety?

These aren't easy questions. But they're the ones that separate leaders who build something real from leaders who just maintain the status quo.

The Long Game

Kirk wasn't the greatest starship captain because he was the smartest or the strongest. He was great because he understood that leadership is about bringing out excellence in others. About trusting them. About leading from the front. About being bold enough to question premises and take calculated risks.

Those lessons don't require a starship. They apply in any organization, in any situation where you're responsible for people and outcomes.

The captain belongs on the bridge. Not directing from a distance. Not hiding in safety. On the bridge, where decisions matter and accountability are visible.

That's where real leadership happens.

That's where trust gets built, where boldness becomes possible, where risk becomes calculated rather than reckless.

If you're going to lead, be the captain on the bridge. Your team—and your organization—will be better for it.

24

The Eager Leader

The Crossing Over

I was reminiscing the first time I became a Team Lead. Not recently. Not in the context of writing about leadership. Just... reminiscing. Thinking back to that moment when you cross over to the other side. When you're no longer "Staff." Now you're "Management."

There was something about that memory that struck me. In my current position as a lead, I've been hitting a wall. Not a crisis. Not a dramatic moment of failure. Just... fatigue. The kind that comes from trying to make even incremental differences to your team, to your organization, and watching the resistance, the inertia, the constraints that make change harder than you thought.

So, I went back. To that first time. To the person who thought, finally, I can make the difference I've been thinking about, dreaming about, complaining about for years.

The Arrival

When you step into that first leadership role, there's a particular kind of energy. It's not just confidence. It's almost euphoria. You've arrived. You've crossed a threshold. The things you couldn't do before—now you can do them.

You walk into your first management meeting with that energy. You're ready. You've been waiting for this moment. You question the decisions that don't make sense. You opine on what could be better. You ideate. You provide solutions. You do all the "...ings" to show you have arrived on the stage.

The ambition is real. The belief is genuine. You've been on the sidelines watching dysfunction, watching missed opportunities, watching people make decisions you would never make. And now you're not on the sidelines anymore. Now you're in the room. Now you have authority. Now you can make the difference you always thought was impossible just by being a regular staff member.

So, you do. You act. You speak up. You push. You try to change things. You can feel it—the possibility. The potential. The window that's finally opened.

Time passes.

When Realism Sets In

And slowly, realism sets in.

Not overnight. Not dramatically. Gradually. You realize that your best idea got watered down in committee. That the change you championed took three times longer than you thought it would. That people didn't follow as enthusiastically as you expected. That organizational gravity is stronger than you anticipated.

You hit resistance you didn't see coming. Politics you didn't understand. Constraints you didn't know existed. People protecting territory. Processes that seem pointless but are harder to change than they should be. Budget limitations. Competing priorities. The reality that your vision, no matter how good, has to fit within systems designed for something else.

And you start to adjust. Not to give up—not exactly. But to adjust your pace. To be more strategic about which battles to fight. To understand that change takes longer. That you need allies. That not everything can be fixed immediately. That sometimes you have to work within the system to change the system.

This is maturity. And it's necessary. It's wisdom. It's the understanding that leadership isn't about having the best ideas—it's about creating conditions where good ideas can take root and grow.

But here's what happens in that journey from eagerness to maturity: you lose something. Not the good judgment. Not the strategic thinking. But something essential gets quieter.

The belief that things can be different. The urgency to try. The conviction that you're supposed to push. The sense that now that you're here, you can actually make it happen.

The Cost of Too Much Realism

After years in leadership, I've watched this happen to many people. They become competent. Effective, even. They navigate complexity well. They make smart decisions. They don't waste energy on impossible battles.

But they also stop trying some things. They accommodate constraints rather than challenging them. They become conservative in their thinking. They stop asking "what if?" and start asking "is this realistic?"

And the organization doesn't get what it actually needs: people in positions of influence who still believe change is possible. Who still push. Who still question. Who still try things that haven't been tried before.

Some of them call this maturity. But I'm not sure it is. I think it might be resignation wearing the costume of wisdom.

The Loop

Here's what I realized: I don't have to choose between that eager person I was and the mature leader I've become. I can be both. Not in a way that makes me reckless or naive. But in a way that keeps me from completely settling into the inertia.

So, I've started deliberately looping back. Remembering that first time. Remembering what that person felt. Remembering the belief that things could be different. Remembering the energy. Remembering the sense of possibility.

And I keep that on a loop. Not because I want to be that person again exactly—I don't want to make that person's mistakes again. But because I need that person's fire. That conviction. That willingness to try.

If I keep this on a loop, I think it might just keep me motivated. Ever on the path to not back down. Ever willing to continue trying. Even when realism whispers that nothing will really change.

Because here's the thing about realism: it's often right. But it's never the full story. The things that did change—the innovations that happened, the cultures that shifted, the people who grew—they happened because someone was willing to stay eager long enough to push through the resistance.

What Maturity Should Actually Mean

Real maturity isn't the loss of eagerness. It's the marriage of eagerness and wisdom. It's staying hungry for change while understanding how change actually happens. It's being ambitious about what's possible while being realistic about constraints.

Real maturity looks like:

Patience with the timeline, urgency about the mission. You understand that change takes time. You're not expecting everything to shift in your first year. But you're also not willing to accept that nothing can shift. You keep pushing, but you've calibrated your expectations about when and how it will happen.

Strategic about battles, but still fighting. You choose which battles to fight. You're not trying to change everything at once. But you're still trying. You're not using constraint as an excuse to stop trying—you're using it to become smarter about how you try.

Mentoring other eager leaders. One of the responsibilities of maturity is protecting that eagerness in the people coming up. Telling them: yes, you'll hit resistance. Yes, change is harder than it looks. But don't let that stop you from trying. Don't trade your eagerness for cynicism.

Building systems that allow change. You can't change everything by force of will. But you can build processes, cultures, structures that make it easier for change to happen. You can reduce friction. You can create space for experimentation. You can make it normal to try things.

Celebrating incremental progress. The mature leader learns that incremental progress matters. Not everything is a home run. A five percent improvement that sticks is worth celebrating. A small cultural shift that spreads is worth noticing. These small things compound over time into real change.

The Person You Were, The Leader You Are

That person who became Team Lead for the first time—they were full of possibility. Naive about obstacles, yes. Underestimating complexity, absolutely. But not wrong about the core thing: that change is possible. That leadership is an opportunity to make a difference. That being in a position of influence means you should try.

The leader you've become—you understand obstacles in ways that person didn't. You've learned what actually works and what doesn't. You've felt the weight of constraints. You've experienced disappointment. You've learned to be strategic.

But you've also lost something. The conviction that you're supposed to push. The belief that your job is to keep trying even when it's hard. The sense that settling for how things are isn't an option.

What if you could have both?

Keeping the Loop Going

I've started asking myself: what would eager-me do right now?

Not to do exactly what that person would do—they'd probably do it wrong, with less wisdom and more bluntness. But to remember their conviction. Their sense of possibility. Their refusal to accept that "this is just how things are."

And I've started doing small things to keep that alive:

Asking "why not?" more than "why?" When someone proposes something new, my instinct is to think about all the reasons it won't work. Instead, I'm trying to ask: what would need to be true for this to work? What would it take?

Pushing back on "that's how we've always done it." This is the death knell of leadership. The moment you accept that historical practice equals current necessity, you've stopped leading. I'm trying to stay suspicious of "we've always done it this way."

Protecting space for experimentation. Remember that chapter on the efficiency illusion? About how organizations mistake meetings for impact? I'm trying to create small spaces where trying new things is actually encouraged. Where failure is information, not career-threatening.

Saying yes to good ideas, even inconvenient ones. The mature move is to shoot down ideas that don't fit the roadmap. The leadership move is to figure out how to make room for good ideas, even when they're inconvenient.

Reminding my team and myself: change is possible. Not easy. Not quick. But possible. We don't have to accept every constraint. We don't have to implement every mandate exactly as handed down. We can find leverage points. We can try different approaches. We can push.

The Danger of Complete Maturity

There's a risk in letting eagerness die completely. The risk is that you become purely adaptive. You respond to what's happening rather than trying to create what you want to happen. You manage rather than lead.

The organizations that succeed aren't the ones with the wisest leaders. They're the ones with leaders who are wise enough to navigate constraints but eager enough to keep pushing against them.

They're the ones where people in positions of influence still believe they're supposed to try. Still ask uncomfortable questions. Still question premises. Still bring ideas that haven't been tried.

If every leader becomes purely mature—purely realistic, purely adaptive—the organization becomes static. It does what it's always done, just slightly better each year.

The Invitation

So, here's what I'm suggesting: don't trade your eagerness for maturity. Integrate them.

Remember what it felt like to cross over. Remember that sense of possibility. Remember the conviction that now that you're here, you could make a difference.

Hold onto that. Not as fantasy. Not as naive belief that change is easy. But as a north star. As a reminder that your job isn't to manage what exists—it's to create what's possible.

Keep that person on a loop. The one who thought they could change things. The one who was willing to try. The one who saw resistance as a puzzle to solve, not a reason to stop trying.

Because the world has enough mature leaders who've adapted to constraints. What it needs is leaders who've learned enough to navigate complexity but still believe strongly enough to push. Leaders who understand that some things won't change—and they accept that. But also believe that some things can change—and they keep trying.

That's not eagerness. That's not maturity. It's both. It's the evolution that makes you actually effective.

The Question for Leaders

As you move through your leadership journey, ask yourself:

- **Have I completely traded eagerness for wisdom?** Or am I finding ways to keep both alive?
- **When was the last time I pushed for something new?** When was the last time I tried something that hadn't been tried before?
- **Am I helping eager leaders stay eager?** Or am I teaching them to become resigned?

- **Do I still believe I'm supposed to make a difference?** Or have I settled into managing what exists?
- **What would eager-me do right now?**

And then maybe, just maybe, do something that person would recognize as leadership.

The Loop

I'm keeping that first time on a loop now. Not to become that person again. But to remember what they knew: that being in a position of influence is an invitation to try. To push. To question. To believe that things can be different.

Maturity taught me how to navigate the system. But eagerness reminds me why I should. Reminds me that my job isn't to accept things as they are. It's to believe they could be different—and then do the work to make that happen.

The person you were when you first stepped into leadership had something real. Don't let maturity completely bury it. Don't trade it for comfort.

Find a way to be both. That's when you actually lead.

25

Motivation in Uncertain Times

The Prelude: When Life Surprises You

Life has a way of surprising you in ways that are either unimaginable or repeat situations from the past. It forces you to stop. Look. Reflect. Revalidate. And move on again.

The pandemic was one of those moments.

We were in quiet good momentum until the first week of March when suddenly news broke: things were not normal. We were facing an adversary that wasn't visible but had the possibility to harm us in ways that could prove fatal to our existence.

We'd been hearing about Corona in our neighbouring country. But for us, the reality was *yahan nahin hai*—it's not here. We were clueless about what needed to be done. Everyone went into query, confusion, cluelessness. Some said, *"mein toh immune hoon"*—I'm immune. Some went into panic mode. Some started seeing masks at the office, maintaining distance, implementing facility measures.

We were not sure how this would affect us personally or at work. We were caught unprepared.

But within that unpreparedness was an opportunity. An opportunity to stop, look, reflect, revalidate. To understand what motivation actually looks like when everything you've relied on disappears.

Part 1: When Decisions Must Be Made in Darkness

The first decision was clear, even in the confusion: personal health and safety of employees and business continuity were the priority.

Within a week, we knew: we had to work from home. The speed at which we had to get teams adjusted with the right infrastructure to carry on their daily activities from home was critical. Remember, lockdown was already in effect in almost every state. There was no time for gradual transition. There was only now.

And here's what mattered: our people were adaptive enough to follow the set directions. They were open enough to dive right into an unexplored world of Work from Home—especially as R&D engineers, we'd never had the possibility to experience this before.

That openness wasn't guaranteed. Teams could have resisted. Could have panicked. Could have checked out. But they didn't. They adapted.

This was the first lesson about motivation in uncertain times: when people understand the priority is their health and safety, when leadership moves decisively even without perfect information, and when teams are invited to adapt rather than ordered to comply—people rise to meet the moment.

Motivation doesn't disappear in crisis. It transforms. It becomes less about individual achievement and more about collective survival. Less about career advancement and more about whether we can actually pull this off together.

Part 2: "I Don't See or Hear You Physically. Are You There?"

We'd never done hardcore R&D design work virtually before. Sure, we knew how to work virtually for routine back-office tasks. We'd done MS Teams calls with partners. But this was different.

Suddenly, our team—the people sitting right next to you, the person whose desk was immediately beside yours, whose conversations happened in real time, who you could turn to and say "look at this"—they were gone. Gone virtually. In the same city maybe, but definitely not next to you.

The challenge was massive. Huge data situations trying to access different applications on home internet. The need for the team to discuss, to exchange ideas, to feed off each other's energy—that physical proximity was gone.

But here's what happened: the team didn't deter. They adapted. We adapted.

This is where motivation in uncertain times gets tested. It's not about the big, inspiring speeches. It's about showing up every day and figuring out how to do work you've never done this way before. It's about the willingness to be imperfect. To try. To fail. To try something different.

Motivation in uncertainty looks like: *What can we actually do right now?* Not *What could we do in a perfect situation?* But *What is possible today, in this moment, with these constraints?*

And the answer, surprisingly, was: quite a lot.

Part 3: When the Invisible Infrastructure Disappears

The basic crux of the workplace is teamwork, networking, and socializing. These are the things that bring out the best in us. The small discussions at the tea vendor. A quick conversation with a friend. A forced encounter with a superior that turns into an insight. The hundreds of small moments that make the workplace special.

Suddenly, all of that was gone.

We missed it. The motivation that came from physical presence, from casual connection, from the energy of people in proximity—it evaporated. Everyone was now only virtual. No video most of the time because people needed to keep their personal situations private.

This is when many teams fall apart. This is when motivation crashes because the infrastructure that sustained it—proximity, casual connection, physical energy—is no longer available.

But something unexpected happened. Thank God for Facebook, WhatsApp, MS Teams, and all the other applications. They became the preparatory instruments that prevented complete breakdown of team connection.

More importantly, the team didn't wait for leadership to figure it out. Team members started creating their own connection points. Informal WhatsApp groups suddenly became the primary source of engagement. Not just work engagement—social engagement. The connection that sustains motivation when physical presence is impossible.

This is crucial: **Motivation in uncertain times isn't something leaders provide. It's something teams create together when given space and tools to do so.**

Part 4: How Do We Keep Motivation Alive?

Kaise motivation zinda rakhein? How do we keep motivation alive?

This is the real question that emerged from the crisis.

The work challenges remained. We'd never been in a situation like this before. The pandemic forced us to reflect on fundamental questions: What defines a regular workplace? Is physical presence required? Is daily commuting to a location in a corner of the city necessary to deliver common goals?

The challenge for managers was different now. We still needed to keep people motivated. But the traditional levers—physical presence, casual connection, visual proximity—they were gone. We had to find new ones.

What we discovered:

Openness and engagement still matter. The openness from team members to engage and interact in this situation was commendable. People still showed up. They still participated. They still cared.

Experimentation becomes essential. We tried things. Sometimes they worked. Sometimes they didn't. We were getting used to trying things differently on a regular basis. That willingness to experiment—to accept that not everything would work but we'd keep trying—that became the culture.

Delegation increases capacity and ownership. With less direct oversight, we delegated more. People took on more responsibilities. And they delivered. Why? Because delegation in uncertain times isn't about monitoring—it's about trust. It's saying: I trust you to figure this out. And people respond to that trust by stepping up.

The informal becomes formal. Before the lockdown, WhatsApp was decent. After the lockdown, it became the primary medium for digital connection in a social manner. That wasn't planned. That wasn't mandated. That was teams finding the tools that worked and using them.

Fun and connection matter more than you think. Spontaneous activities started happening: riddles, quizzes on daily basis. Weekend team challenges: "WFH selfies at our home workplaces," "We became MasterChef," "Fastest picture first," "Fitness challenge," online games of housie. These weren't replacing the tea vendor conversations. But they were creating connection in a different form.

Recognition of effort matters. Reviews had to be balanced differently. People were already engaging heavily on a day-to-day basis. The recognition came not from traditional performance metrics but from acknowledging that people were showing up, trying, contributing ideas for how to make remote work actually work.

The Real Discovery: Shared Responsibility for Motivation

What I came to realize is this: keeping motivation up isn't just the leader's responsibility.

This is a radical shift from traditional thinking. We imagine motivation as something leaders provide. But in uncertain times, motivation becomes a shared responsibility. Team members contribute with ideas and solutions for effective working from home. They share the work pressures. They're patient and try out options to make things work.

The sheer fact that we were able to adapt and still keep business continuity shows something real: commitment and motivation with each team member. Each member of the team, in their own way, is making the extra effort to keep the motivation and morale of the team up.

This is what the pandemic taught us: **In times of real uncertainty, when the traditional infrastructure of motivation disappears, teams that survive are the ones where everyone understands they're responsible for motivation. Not just the leader. Everyone.**

What Actually Motivates in Uncertain Times

The pandemic stripped away a lot of the noise about motivation. No amount of team-building exercises could replace the absence of physical presence. No motivational speeches could overcome the fear and uncertainty.

What actually motivated people:

Clarity about priorities. We knew: health and safety first. Business continuity second. Everything else was secondary. That clarity, even in the chaos, gave people something to hold onto.

Decisiveness, even with incomplete information. We didn't wait for perfect data. We made decisions. We moved to WFH. We figured out infrastructure. We adapted. That decisiveness—showing that leadership was taking action even without perfect information—reassured people. It meant someone was at the helm.

Permission to be human. People weren't expected to pretend everything was normal. They weren't expected to be "on" all the time. Video off was okay. Personal situations being private was okay. The acknowledgment that this was hard, unusual, and required grace—that mattered.

Shared struggle. Everyone was in this together. The senior leader was in a home office. The junior engineer was in a home office. The challenge was collective. That shared experience of being in the same boat—that created something that normal organizational hierarchy couldn't create.

Trust that was tested and held up. People were working from home with minimal supervision. The organization trusted them to do their work. And they delivered. That mutual trust—tested by unprecedented circumstances and holding up—that became the foundation of new motivation.

Connection that people created themselves. Leadership provided the tools and permission. But teams created the connection through WhatsApp groups, through spontaneous fun activities, through looking out for each other. That organic connection mattered more than any official team-building program.

When Traditional Motivation Breaks

The crisis revealed something about traditional motivation frameworks: they often don't hold up in real uncertainty.

Performance incentives become meaningless when job security is uncertain. Career advancement feels irrelevant when you're worried about health. Individual recognition falls flat when people are exhausted and isolated.

What holds up is simpler and more profound:

- Knowing that your health matters to the organization
- Understanding the shared mission and why it matters
- Experiencing trust from leadership
- Feeling connected to your team
- Seeing that leadership is also navigating this, not hiding from it
- Being given autonomy to figure out how to do your work in new conditions

These aren't motivational tactics. These are the foundations of real motivation—the things that matter when everything else falls away.

The Maturity That Comes from Crisis

The pandemic helped us mature as a team. It wasn't optional maturity. It was forced maturity. We had to adapt or we couldn't function. We had to trust or we couldn't work remotely. We had to stay connected or we'd fragment.

And in going through that forced maturation together, something shifted. The team came together at a different level. Not because of shared experiences of success or celebration, but because of shared experiences of challenge and adaptation.

That's a bond that typical workplace experiences don't create.

Lessons for Leading in Any Uncertain Time

The pandemic wasn't unique in creating uncertainty. It was just particularly intense. But any major change—reorganization, market disruption, leadership transition, loss of a major client—creates uncertainty.

The lessons from the pandemic apply:

Clarity about what matters most. Health, safety, continuity—the fundamentals. Strip away everything else and get clear about priorities.

Decisiveness even with incomplete information. People can handle not knowing everything. They can't handle leaders who are paralyzed. Move. Adjust. Move again.

Permission for people to adapt their own way. You can't control how people adapt. You can create space for them to figure it out.

Transparency about what you don't know. Say it: "We don't know how long this will last." "We're figuring this out as we go." "I don't have all the answers." That honesty is motivating because it's real.

Distribution of responsibility. Motivation isn't something leaders inject into teams. It's something teams create together when given autonomy and connection.

Connection as a primary focus. When everything else is unstable, connection becomes essential. Whether it's through informal channels, spontaneous activities, or just regular one-on-ones where you check in on the person, not just the work.

Recognition of effort, not just results. In uncertain times, the effort matters more than the outcome because outcomes are uncertain. Recognize that people are showing up, trying, contributing.

The Question for Leaders

As you navigate uncertain times:

- **Are you clear about the fundamentals?** Health, safety, continuity. What else is truly essential?
- **Are you being decisive or waiting for perfect information?** People need leadership, not paralysis.

- **Are you trying to motivate people, or are you creating conditions where they can motivate themselves?** Big difference.
- **Are you being transparent about what you don't know?** Honesty is motivating because it's real.
- **Are you recognizing effort and adaptation, or just measuring outcomes?** Outcomes are uncertain. Effort is visible.
- **Are you staying connected to your team?** Not just for updates, but for real connection?

The Lessons We're Forgetting

The pandemic was brutal. It was disruptive. It forced us into situations none of us wanted to be in.

But it also revealed something important about motivation: it's not fragile. It's resilient. It doesn't depend on physical presence or perfect conditions. It depends on clarity, trust, connection, and shared purpose.

When those things are present—even in crisis, especially in crisis—people stay motivated. Not with the enthusiasm of an eager leader in their first role. But with the deeper motivation that comes from knowing they're part of something that matters, that they're trusted to figure it out, that they're connected to people who have their back.

That's the motivation that carries through uncertain times. That's the motivation that doesn't need perfect conditions to survive.

But here's what's disappointing: even after we've gone through the crisis, even after we've learned the most important lessons about working remotely, being responsible, delivering with accountability, adapting to virtual methods more effectively and efficiently—organizations are still reverting to full-time office presence.

Please don't get me wrong. I understand the challenges. Hierarchy has their own constraints: policies, government regulations, capital investments, office spaces that need to be justified. I'm not blind to the complexity.

But we were given an opportunity. And we did quite well. We proved something real:

- People can be trusted with their tasks to be managed more on their own
- Cost efficiency can be maintained without sacrificing quality or commitment
- Accountability doesn't require physical presence
- Innovation and collaboration can happen virtually with the right tools and culture
- Teams can be stronger, more connected, more resilient working remotely than they were in the office

We learned this not in theory, but in practice. Under pressure. In crisis. When there was no time for debate. We had to do it. And we did.

And now, instead of building on what could have led to a different and much more opportunistically better approach, these learnings are being wasted.

The Opportunity Slipping Away

This is the tragedy: organizations are taking the lessons of the pandemic and burying them.

They're not building on the trust that was built. They're reverting to old models of control and presence. They're asking people to commute again, to sit in offices, to perform presence for people who've learned to manage without seeing them.

They're taking the cost efficiencies they discovered and abandoning them. They're losing the flexibility they learned to build. They're going backwards.

And the people who led through the crisis, who adapted, who built new cultures of trust and accountability—many of them are leaving. Because they've experienced something different now. They know it's possible. And they're not willing to go back to the old way just because it's more comfortable for leadership.

The missed opportunity is profound. We had a chance to fundamentally reshape how organizations work. We had proof that it was possible. We had momentum.

And we're squandering it.

Why This Matters for Leadership

This is worth noting because it reveals something about organizational maturity and leadership courage.

The organizations that learned from the pandemic and are building on those lessons—they'll attract and retain talent. They'll innovate faster. They'll be more resilient. They'll adapt better to the next disruption.

The organizations that revert to the old ways will lose their best people. The ones who've experienced autonomy, trust, and effectiveness working remotely. The ones who've proven they don't need office presence to deliver.

This is a leadership test. Not just in crisis, but in recovery. Can leaders take what they learned and build on it? Can they resist the pull to go back to "how we've always done things"? Can they defend the new approaches they discovered when pressured to return to the old?

Some will. Many won't.

And the ones who don't—who give up on the lessons of the pandemic the moment the crisis eases—they'll be making a critical mistake.

The Real Question

The real question isn't whether people can work remotely. We've proven they can. The question is: do leaders have the courage to build differently?

To trust the lessons, they learned when crisis forced them to? To maintain the flexibility and autonomy that emerged? To resist the pressure to return to control-based, presence-based models of management?

Or will they take what was forced upon them during the pandemic—what we discovered we could actually do—and file it away as "that was an emergency, now we're back to normal"?

If it's the latter, we'll have wasted perhaps the most significant leadership lesson of our generation: that the way we thought we needed to work wasn't actually necessary. That people are more capable than we thought. That trust actually works. That accountability doesn't require surveillance.

Don't Waste the Gift

For leaders still navigating the return-to-office pressure: Don't waste what you learned.

You learned that people can be trusted. Don't go back to requiring presence to prove they're working.

You learned that accountability works without constant oversight. Don't revert to visible-presence management.

You learned that virtual connection is possible and meaningful. Don't use return-to-office as an excuse to undo the flexibility you built.

You learned that cost efficiency and employee autonomy can coexist. Don't sacrifice those learnings for the comfort of the traditional office model.

The pandemic gave us an involuntary experiment in what organizations could actually look like. What we learned was real. What we proved was real.

The question now is: will we be brave enough to build on it? Or will we waste the opportunity and go back to the way things were, pretending we didn't learn anything?

The answer to that question will define leadership in the post-pandemic era.

26

Why Strong Leadership is Rare

The Paradox

We know what strong leadership looks like. We've written books about it. We've trained leaders on it. We've created frameworks, models, competencies. Organizations invest millions in leadership development.

Yet strong leadership remains rare.

Not because people don't want it. Not because it's impossible. But because the systems we've built actually select against it, reward the opposite, and then wonder why we don't have it.

This is the paradox at the heart of modern organizations: we claim to value strong leadership while systematically rewarding weak leadership. We say we want integrity while incentivizing deception. We say we want long-term health while measuring only short-term results.

And then we're surprised when scandals emerge. When talented people leave. When cultures become toxic. When organizations collapse under the weight of problems that should have been caught and fixed years earlier.

The issue isn't that strong leaders don't exist. The issue is that the systems we've created make it nearly impossible for them to thrive, and make it very comfortable for weak leaders to flourish.

The Four Systemic Issues That Kill Strong Leadership

1. Short-Term Incentives Dominate

Executives are judged on results. Not long-term health. Not sustainable value. Not whether the organization is actually getting better. Results. This quarter. This year.

That creates a perverse incentive structure: maximize short-term results at the expense of long-term health.

A strong leader would say: "We need to invest in culture, even though it costs us this quarter." A weak leader says: "We need to hit our numbers, even if it means cutting corners and hiding problems."

The system rewards the weak leader. They hit their targets. They move up. They get promoted. And when problems surface later—when the corners they cut come back to haunt the organization—they're long gone. They're the problem of the next leader.

This is the mechanism: short-term incentives don't just encourage weak leadership. They actively punish strong leadership. A strong leader who invests in the long term often appears weak in the short term. Their numbers aren't as impressive. Their approach looks inefficient. And they get passed over for the person who cut corners and hit the targets.

The result? Organizations fill their leadership pipeline with people who got ahead by optimizing for the wrong timeline. And then they're shocked when those people run the organization into the ground long-term.

2. Fear-Based Cultures Normalize Deception

In organizations where mistakes aren't safe to admit, people hide them. Not because they're bad people. But because they're rational. Because admitting a mistake could cost them their job, their reputation, their advancement.

So, mistakes get buried. Problems get hidden. Red flags get ignored because surfacing them might make you look bad.

And over time, this gets normalized. It becomes "how things work." People stop seeing it as dysfunction. It becomes culture. It becomes "this is just what it's like to work here."

I've seen this in organization after organization: a problem that could have been caught and fixed early—if people felt safe surfacing it—becomes a catastrophic problem because it was hidden for years. By the time it surfaces, the damage is massive. But the people who hid it? They're fine. They're not held accountable because the culture made hiding it safe and normal.

This is how organizations fail. Not in dramatic moments. But in the slow normalization of deception. In the fear-based systems that incentivize lying about status, hiding problems, and misrepresenting reality.

A strong leader creates safety for honest reporting. But in a fear-based culture, that strong leader gets undermined by the system. Subordinates don't trust them. They've learned that admitting problems gets punished. So, they tell strong leaders what strong leaders want to hear, not what's actually true.

3. Misaligned Accountability

If senior leadership faces no real consequences for deception or ethical lapses, bad behaviour gets modelled from the top.

This is simple but profound: accountability flows downward. If the CEO can get away with misrepresenting results and faces no consequence, then executives below them can too. If executives can hide problems and still get promoted, then managers can too.

Accountability isn't about punishment. It's about consistency. It's about everyone understanding that there are consequences for breaching ethics, for deception, for choices that prioritize personal gain over organizational health.

When accountability is absent at the top, everything that comes below is performative. Rules are for other people. Ethics are for people without power.

I've watched organizations where senior leaders explicitly stated values they didn't live by. Where they preached integrity while engaging in deception. Where they talked about psychological safety while punishing people who spoke up.

And they did this openly. Not hidden. Openly. Because they knew there would be no consequences. Governance looked the other way. The board was asleep. Shareholders only cared about profits.

So, executives modelled bad behaviour. And middle managers saw it and thought: if the top is doing this, why shouldn't I? And they did. And the culture normalized it.

By the time it gets to frontline teams, deception and corner-cutting are just "how we work here."

4. Corporate Governance Looks the Other Way

As long as profits are up, red flags get ignored.

This is where accountability truly breaks down. The board's job is to ensure the organization is being run ethically and sustainably. But many boards are asleep. Or complicit. Or both.

They see warning signs: high turnover, ethical concerns, accounting irregularities, complaints about leadership. And they look the other way. Because profits are up. Because the stock is rising. Because questioning it might be uncomfortable.

Until they can't. Until the problem gets so big that ignoring it becomes impossible. Until a scandal explodes or the organization collapses.

And then there's hand-wringing. "How did this happen?" "We had no idea." "We need to investigate."

But they did have ideas. The signs were there. They just chose not to see them because seeing them would require action, and action would be uncomfortable.

This is where strong leadership absolutely cannot survive. A strong leader needs governance that's actually paying attention. That holds them accountable. That surfaces issues. That protects the organization's long-term health even when it's uncomfortable.

When governance abdicates that responsibility, strong leaders can't operate. The system doesn't support them. In fact, the system actively works against them.

The Cost of "Easy Way Out" Leadership

When organizations accept weak leadership because it's easier than demanding strong leadership, the costs are severe.

Erodes internal trust and morale. People see through it. They know when leadership is making decisions based on personal gain rather than organizational good. They know when leaders are hiding problems. They know when accountability isn't real. And they stop trusting. They stop believing that the organization is actually trying to do good work. They become cynical. They disengage.

Increases risk of scandals. Problems that should have been fixed early fester. They grow. They compound. Until they cxplode. And then there's a scandal. Reputational damage. Regulatory investigation. The organization suffers massive damage that could have been prevented if problems had been surfaced and fixed early.

Damages long-term stakeholder value. Shareholders think weak leadership is profitable short-term. But it destroys value long-term. Customers lose trust. Employees leave. Regulators investigate. What looked profitable short-term becomes destructive long-term.

Drives away the very people who could make the company better. The strong leaders. The ones with integrity. The ones who care about long-term health. They see the system rewards the opposite of what they believe in. And they leave. They go to organizations where their values align with the system. They don't stick around to fight a rigged game.

And the organization is left with people who've thrived in a system that rewards weak leadership. Which only makes the system worse.

Why This Matters Across Every Chapter in This Book

Everything I've written about in this book—ego, trust, psychological safety, governance, loyalty vs. competence, innovation, burnout, motivation—all of it requires strong leadership to actually work.

But strong leadership can't emerge from weak systems.

You can't build psychological safety in a fear-based culture. You can't create accountability when accountability isn't real at the top. You can't build trust when leaders are routinely deceptive. You can't empower people to innovate when mistakes aren't safe. You can't develop loyalty based on merit when loyalty to people matters more than competence.

All of the practices I've described in this book—they only work in organizations that have actually decided to support strong leadership. That have aligned their systems, incentives, and accountability structures to reward it.

Most organizations haven't made that decision. They've made the opposite decision: optimized for short-term results, accepted fear-based cultures, misaligned accountability, and a board that looks the way.

And then they're confused why strong leadership is rare.

What's Required (Slowly, But...)

The good news is that pressure is mounting. And change is beginning to happen. Slowly. Unevenly. But it's happening.

Stakeholder capitalism is pushing more focus on integrity.

The old model—maximize shareholder value at all costs—is being challenged. Increasingly, investors, customers, employees, and communities are demanding that organizations consider a broader set of stakeholders. That means long-term health matters again. That means integrity matters. That means weak leadership that destroys value long-term is no longer acceptable.

This creates space for strong leaders. Because strong leadership is increasingly aligned with value creation—long-term value, not just short-term results.

Whistleblower protections are getting stronger.

When people can safely report problems without retaliation, problems surface early. When problems surface early, they get fixed. When problems get fixed early, they don't become scandals.

Stronger whistleblower protections mean fear-based cultures can't work the way they used to. Deception becomes harder. Accountability becomes more real.

This creates pressure on organizations to actually build psychologically safe cultures. Because hiding problems becomes riskier than surfacing them.

Employees and customers are now demanding transparency.

People have options. They can work anywhere. They can do business with anyone. And increasingly, they're choosing to work for and do business with organizations that are honest. That are ethical. That actually try to do right by their stakeholders.

This is a market force. And market forces drive change faster than anything else.

When your top talent is leaving because the culture is toxic, when your customers are going to competitors because they trust them more, when your reputation is suffering because you cut corners—that's when organizations finally get serious about strong leadership.

Leadership development programs are starting to emphasize emotional intelligence, ethics, and governance—not just results.

Slowly, the industry is recognizing that technical competence isn't enough. That results without integrity are toxic. That long-term leadership requires emotional intelligence, ethical grounding, and understanding of governance.

This is a start. It's not universal. But it's movement in the right direction.

What Organizations Need to Do

If an organization actually wants strong leadership, here's what needs to change:

Align incentives with long-term health. Stop measuring leaders only on quarterly results. Start measuring them on culture, retention, ethical conduct, long-term stakeholder value. Make it clear that short-term results at the expense of long-term health won't be tolerated.

Build psychological safety from the top. Senior leaders need to model it. They need to admit mistakes. They need to ask for help. They need to create an environment where honesty is safe. And they need to be protected by governance that doesn't punish them for surfacing problems.

Implement real accountability. Make it clear that everyone—including senior leaders—faces consequences for ethical breaches, deception, and corner-cutting. Make accountability consistent. Make it visible. Make it real.

Activate the board. Governance needs to move from rubber-stamp to actually paying attention. Ask hard questions. Require transparency. Surface issues that might be uncomfortable. Protect long-term organizational health even when it's unpopular short-term.

Develop leaders explicitly. Don't just promote people who got ahead by cutting corners. Invest in developing people who can lead with integrity. Mentor them. Coach them. Support them. Make it clear that strong leadership is what you're looking for.

Reward strong leadership visibly. When a leader makes a choice that's right long-term but hurts short-term results, celebrate it. When a leader surfaces a problem instead of hiding it, promote them. When a leader develops people and builds culture, make it clear that matters.

Make it obvious what the organization actually values, not what it says it values.

The Choice Organizations Face

This is where we are: organizations can continue to optimize for short-term results, fear-based cultures, misaligned accountability, and governance that looks the other way. And they can continue to be surprised that strong leadership is rare.

Or they can make a different choice.

They can decide that long-term health matters. That integrity matters. That strong leadership is actually what they want. And then they can align their systems, incentives, and accountability to make it possible.

The second path is harder. It requires discipline. It requires governance paying attention. It requires senior leaders being vulnerable. It requires sometimes sacrificing short-term results for long-term value.

But it's the path that creates organizations where strong leadership actually thrives. Where talented people stay. Where problems surface early and get fixed. Where culture is healthy. Where long-term value actually compounds.

For Leaders Operating in Weak Systems

If you're a strong leader in an organization with weak systems, you're in a difficult position. You're trying to build psychologically safe teams in a fear-based culture. You're trying to develop people based on merit when the organization rewards loyalty to powerful people. You're trying to create accountability when accountability isn't real.

You can do some of this. You can create psychological safety in your span of influence. You can develop people well. You can hold your team accountable. You can model strong leadership.

But you're fighting against the system. And over time, that gets exhausting.

My advice: do what you can within your sphere. But also recognize the limits. Some systems are too broken to fix from the middle. Some organizations have made choices that are incompatible with strong leadership. And at some point, the choice becomes: do I stay and keep fighting a rigged game, or do I go find an organization where the system actually supports strong leadership?

Both are valid choices. But don't pretend a broken system will suddenly become healthy if you just work harder. It won't. Systems change when organizations make a choice to change them.

The Invitation

If you lead an organization: make a choice. Actually, make it. Decide that strong leadership matters. And then change the systems to support it.

Stop measuring only short-term results. Start creating psychological safety. Start implementing real accountability. Start activating your board. Start developing leaders for the long term.

It won't be quick. It won't be easy. But it's possible.

And the organizations that make that choice? They'll have something increasingly rare: strong leaders who stay. Who develops others. Who builds culture. Who create long-term value.

That's where competitive advantage actually lives. Not in short-term results. In the strength of leadership and the health of the organization that leadership builds.

Strong leadership is rare because systems don't support it. But that doesn't have to be true. Organizations can make a different choice.

The question is: will they?

Part – VII
Closing Reflections

27

Leadership Is Protection, Not Projection

The Core Responsibility

My leadership priority has always been simple: ensure that the people I lead feel represented, protected, and secure under my leadership.

Not results. Not metrics. Not personal advancement. Those matter, but they're secondary. The primary thing is that the people who've chosen to work with me know that I have their back. That I will stand for them. That when things get difficult, they're not alone.

It's not just about results. It's about standing up for your team, especially when things don't go as planned.

This is where the real test of leadership happens. Not in moments of success. Anyone can look good when things are going well. The test comes when something breaks. When a project fails. When targets aren't met. When something goes wrong.

That's when you discover what kind of leader you actually are.

The Deflection Trap

Too often, I've watched blame get unfairly shifted onto staff when targets aren't met. A leader takes credit for success. Then when something goes wrong, suddenly it's the team's fault. Suddenly it's a resource issue.

Suddenly it's external factors. Suddenly the leader is explaining why this failure isn't their responsibility.

That's not leadership. That's deflection.

I've seen smart people, talented people, broken by this kind of leadership. They deliver, they're invisible. Something goes wrong, suddenly they're visible—as the scapegoat.

And the leader? The leader is fine. The leader's career is fine. The leader's reputation is fine. Because they managed to distance themselves from the failure.

This is where organizations become toxic. Not through evil intent. But through leaders who've mastered the art of protecting themselves and leaving their teams exposed.

The Owner's Stance

As leaders, we must own the outcome. Whether success or failure.

This doesn't mean you ignore individual or collective contributions. Of course those matter. Some people perform better than others. Some teams deliver better results than others. That's real and it should be recognized.

But the outcome—the results, the success, the failure—that's owned by the leader. First. Not shared. Not distributed. Owned.

A strong leader looks at a successful project and says: "My team delivered this. I created the conditions for them to succeed." A strong leader looks at a failed project and says: "This is my failure. I either didn't provide the right support, didn't set clear direction, didn't shield them from chaos, or made a bad decision. I own this."

Even when results are driven by collective or individual contributions—both the brilliant work of a team member and the failure of another team member—the leader must step forward first. Not hide behind the team. Not distribute blame. Not distance themselves from the outcome.

Step forward. Own it. That's what leaders do.

Representation without Responsibility Is Hollow

Here's what hollow leadership looks like: claiming to lead "X number of people" without actually representing their best interests when it matters most.

I've seen leaders who talk about their teams constantly. Who brag about their reports. Who make big speeches about how much they care about people. But when push comes to shove, when there's political pressure from above, when standing up for the team might cost them something—suddenly they're nowhere to be found.

Representation without responsibility is just a title. It's not leadership.

Real representation means: when your team member makes a mistake, you don't throw them under the bus to appease your boss. You own the mistake. You explain what happened. You take responsibility. And then you help them learn and do better.

Real representation means: when your team is under attack from organizational politics, you don't stay silent to stay safe. You speak up. You defend them. You advocate for them. Even if it's uncomfortable. Even if it costs you politically.

Real representation means: when a decision from above will harm your team, you push back. You make the case for why this is a bad idea. You don't just implement it and then blame upper management.

Real representation is active. It's courageous. It's putting your team's interests ahead of your own comfort.

Most leaders don't do this. Most leaders protect themselves first. And that's understandable—self-preservation is powerful. But it's not leadership. It's survival.

Shielding From Toxicity, Enabling Growth

Leadership is about shielding your team from unnecessary toxicity. Not all toxicity. Some friction is healthy. Some challenge is necessary. But the toxicity that comes from organizational dysfunction, from leadership failures above, from unnecessary chaos—that's what you shield your team from.

You do this by:

- Taking the heat from above so it doesn't reach your team
- Managing the noise so your team can focus on real work
- Buffering them from political battles that aren't theirs to fight
- Creating psychological safety so they can take risks
- Protecting them when they fail in service of growth

But shielding from toxicity isn't about creating a bubble. It's not about protecting them from all difficulty. It's about protecting them so they can grow.

Because growth happens at the edge of challenge. It happens when people take risks. When they try things. When they fail and learn. When they push themselves.

A protective leader creates the conditions where people can grow. That means removing unnecessary obstacles. It means shielding them from toxicity. But it also means challenging them. Pushing them. Requiring more from them than they thought was possible.

The protection isn't about making things comfortable. It's about making things possible.

The Culture of Accountability, Not Fear

Too many organizations have confused accountability with fear. They think if people are afraid—afraid of making mistakes, afraid of being blamed, afraid of consequences—then they'll perform better.

It's the opposite.

Fear makes people hide. Fear makes people play it safe. Fear makes people optimize for not getting caught rather than for doing good work. Fear kills the very things that make organizations work: honesty, risk-taking, innovation, engagement.

Real accountability is different. It's about clear expectations. It's about consequences—both positive and negative. It's about following through on what you said. It's about making decisions based on merit and outcome, not on who has the most political power.

A protective leader creates accountability, not fear. They make it clear what's expected. They follow through on consequences. They're consistent. But they also create psychological safety so that people can admit mistakes, can ask for help, can take intelligent risks without career-threatening consequences.

That's accountability. That's what actually drives performance.

Fear-based accountability drives compliance and deception. Real accountability drives commitment and honesty.

Standing For, Not Behind

This is the crucial distinction: standing for your team, not behind them.

Standing behind means: the team is in front, taking the heat. The leader is safe, protected, ready to run if necessary. The leader says "my team" but positions themselves as separate from the team's outcomes. Ready to blame them if things go wrong, ready to claim credit if things go well.

Standing for means: the leader is visible. The leader is on the line. The leader is saying: this is my team, these are our results, and I own them. You want to blame someone for failure? Start with me. You want to credit someone with success? Credit my team, but know that the buck stops with me.

It's not about being heroic or self-sacrificing. It's about being honest about the nature of leadership. You have authority. Authority comes with responsibility. That responsibility means your name is on the outcomes.

Some leaders find this terrifying. Because it means you're exposed. Because it means your failures are visible. Because it means you can't hide.

But that's the deal of leadership. You get authority. In exchange, you get accountability. You get exposure. You get risk.

If you're not willing to take that deal, don't be a leader. Be an individual contributor. Be an expert. Be something where you're not responsible for other people.

But if you take the deal—if you step into leadership—then step forward. Stand for your team. Own the outcomes. Don't hide behind them.

The Cost of Protection

I won't pretend this doesn't cost something. Standing for your team when there's pressure to deflect—that's a choice. It's a choice that might damage your reputation in some circles. It's a choice that might slow your advancement in some organizations. It's a choice that might make you unpopular with certain people.

But it's a choice that builds something real: loyalty. Trust. A team that knows they have a leader who will stand with them. A culture where people aren't paranoid. A place where excellence can actually happen because people aren't spending all their energy protecting themselves politically.

The cost is real. But so is the benefit.

And over time, if you consistently stand for your team, you'll find that the people who matter—your team, your peers who have integrity, your leaders who actually have principles—those people will respect you more. They'll follow you more willingly. They'll work harder for you.

You might lose some people who only respect power politics and ruthlessness. Good. You probably don't want to work with them anyway.

But you'll attract and retain the best people. The ones who are looking for a leader who actually has their back. The ones who want to do excellent work because they trust their leader. The ones who will follow you across organizations because they know what it means to work for someone who stands for them.

What Protection Actually Looks Like

Protection isn't abstract. It looks like something. Let me be specific.

When a team member makes a mistake: You own it first. You explain what happened to your leadership. You explain the context. You explain what you'll do differently. You take responsibility. Then, privately, you talk to the team member. You understand what happened. You help them learn. You move forward.

You don't say: "My team member did this." You say: "This happened under my watch. Here's how we're going to fix it."

When your team is unfairly blamed: You speak up. You provide context. You defend them publicly. You make it clear that the blame is misplaced. You explain what actually happened. And you do this even if it's politically uncomfortable.

When decisions from above will harm your team: You push back. You make the case for why this is a bad idea. If the decision stands, you explain it to your team as clearly as possible. But you try. You don't just implement bad decisions and pretend they're your team's fault.

When a team member is developing and makes a choice you disagree with: You let them make it. You provide input. But if they're confident and it's not reckless, you let them own the decision. You protect them from unnecessary consequences if it doesn't work out. Because growth requires the freedom to fail.

When organizational toxicity threatens your team: You create a buffer. You shield them from it. You give them a place where they can do good work even if the organization around them is dysfunctional.

When a team member is struggling: You protect their confidence. You provide support. You don't broadcast their struggles to others. You help them get back on track privately. You don't use their struggle as evidence that they're weak or incapable.

This is what protection looks like. It's active. It's intentional. It's risky. But it's what builds trust.

For Leaders Who've Been Burned

If you've stood for your team before and it cost you—if you took a bullet for someone and they didn't recognize it, or worse, they threw you under the bus later—I understand if you're cautious now.

But here's what I've learned: you cannot pick and choose the way you protect people.

Yes, some people may be disloyal. Yes, some will disappoint you. Yes, some won't reciprocate with commitment. That's real. That hurts. And it's tempting to say: I'll protect the loyal ones, the grateful ones, the ones who deserve it.

But that's not protection. That's favouritism. That's conditional care. And the moment you start conditioning protection on loyalty or gratitude, you've fundamentally changed what protection is.

Real protection is unconditional. You protect all of your team. Not because they've earned it. Not because they're grateful. But because they're your team. Because as a leader, that's your responsibility.

Now, protection doesn't mean they stay forever. It doesn't mean enabling dysfunction or tolerating disloyalty indefinitely. It means this: you still stand by them. You still have the honest conversation. You still see them as a whole person, not just as a problem.

If someone is disloyal, if there's a fundamental misalignment, if it's clear they expect something different or want something else—then as a leader, you have a heart-to-heart conversation. You understand what's driving it. You help them see the reality. And if the best path forward is for them to move on, you support that transition with dignity and care.

But throughout that process, you're still protecting them. You're still standing for them. You're not throwing them under the bus to protect yourself or to appease the rest of the team. You're helping them make the best decision for them and for the organization.

That's the difference: you can protect someone while also helping them move to a place where they'll be better served. You can stand for someone while acknowledging that they might not be the right fit for your team.

The protection is unconditional. The employment relationship might need to change. But the protection—the willingness to see them as a person, to treat them with dignity, to stand by them in the conversation—that's unconditional.

Because the moment you start saying "some people aren't worth protecting," you've lost something essential. You've made protection transactional. You've made it about who deserves it rather than about what leadership is.

And then you're just another leader looking out for themselves and their favourites. The alternative—a culture where leaders protect themselves and leave their teams exposed—is worse. It's corrosive. It's toxic. It's not leadership.

But protection that only applies to loyal people? That's not much better. That's just loyalty-based leadership wearing a different mask.

True protection is for everyone. Even the people who disappoint you. Even the people who don't reciprocate. Even the people you eventually help move on to a better place.

That's the standard. That's what separates leaders who actually have principles from leaders who just talk about them.

The Question for Leaders

Ask yourself:

- **When something goes wrong in my team, what's my instinct?** To explain and defend, or to distance and deflect?
- **Do my people know I have their back?** Or do they wonder if I'll throw them under the bus?
- **Am I standing for my team or behind them?** Am I visible when it matters, or do I hide?
- **Do I own outcomes, or do I distribute blame?** When something succeeds, who gets credit? When something fails, who takes responsibility?
- **Am I building a culture of accountability or fear?** Are people honest about problems, or are they hiding?
- **If I had to take a hit for my team, would I?** Or would I rationalize why it's their responsibility, not mine?

These aren't easy questions. But they're the questions that define what kind of leader you actually are.

The Legacy of Protective Leadership

Leaders who protect their teams build something that lasts.

They build loyalty. Not the forced kind that comes from fear or obligation. The real kind that comes from knowing someone has your back.

They build psychological safety. People can admit mistakes because they know the response will be learning, not punishment. People can take risks because they know their leader will support them.

They build high performance. Because people who trust their leader will run through walls for them. They'll work harder. They'll stay longer. They'll care more about the mission.

They build cultures where excellence is possible. Because people aren't spending all their energy on politics and self-protection. They're focused on the actual work.

And when they move on—when they leave the organization or get promoted—their team carries that experience with them. They expect leadership that protects. They build it in their own teams. They perpetuate it.

That's how cultures change. Not through mandates from above. But through leaders who, day after day, stand for their teams. Who owns outcomes. Who shield from toxicity. Who create accountability instead of fear.

The Final Principle

Leadership is not projection. It's not about making yourself look good. It's not about positioning yourself ahead of your team. It's not about advancing your career by being visible while your team is invisible.

Leadership is protection.

It's standing up. It's standing forward. It's being visible when it matters. It's owning outcomes. It's representing your team's best interests. It's creating conditions where people can do their best work.

It's taking the risk that comes with authority.

If you're not willing to do that, don't claim to be a leader. Because the deal of leadership is this: you get authority, you get power, you get influence. In exchange, you're responsible. You're accountable. You're exposed.

The question isn't whether that's fair. The question is: are you willing to take the deal?

If you are, then protect your team. Stand for them. Own the outcomes. Build a culture where people know their leader has their back.

That's leadership. Everything else is just management wearing a different title.

28

Final Thought - Empowerment > Micromanagement

Where we've Been

We've covered a lot of ground in this book. We've talked about persistence and resignation. About ego and humility. About burnout and breakthrough. About psychological safety and speaking up. About innovation in constrained systems. About the gap between potential and performance. About governance and accountability. About loyalty and competence. About protection and projection.

Each chapter has been a piece of a larger puzzle. Each insight has been a thread in a larger tapestry.

But if you strip away all the complexity, if you reduce everything down to its essence, it comes to this: the difference between leaders who build something real and leaders who just manage what exists is this fundamental choice—empowerment or micromanagement.

Everything else flows from that choice.

The Greatest Results

One of the greatest results I've seen as a leader is when I've empowered team members to take full ownership of their deliverables.

Not responsibility with restrictions. Not authority with asterisks. Full ownership. The whole thing. From conception through delivery through evaluation.

And yes, they may stumble. Yes, the path may not always be perfect. Yes, there will be moments where you think, "If I had just stepped in and done this myself, it would have been faster/better/cleaner."

You'd probably be right. In the short term.

But that's not the measure. The measure is what happens over time. What happens to the person. What happens to their capability. What happens to their confidence. What happens to the culture.

And what happens consistently in my experience is this: the person grows. They become capable of things they didn't think they could do. They discover capacities they didn't know they had. They become someone different—more confident, more skilled, more willing to take on challenge.

And the work improves. Not immediately. But over time. Because they own it. Because they're not executing someone else's vision—they're creating their own. Because there's no one else to blame if it doesn't work out, so they're invested in making it work.

This is what real empowerment looks like.

The Paradox of Letting Go

Here's the paradox that most micromanagers miss: empowerment isn't about letting go.

Empowerment is about trusting growth.

Micromanagement comes from a place of control. From a belief that if you don't oversee every decision, every step, every detail, things will fall apart. That you need to maintain visibility and control to ensure quality.

It often comes from a good place—fear that things won't go right, that people will fail, that if you're not watching, problems will emerge. It comes from caring about the work, about the outcomes.

But it's based on a false premise: that your constant oversight prevents failure. In reality, it prevents something far more important—the growth that comes from people figuring things out themselves.

Empowerment is different. Empowerment comes from a belief that people are capable. That they want to do good work. That given space and support, they'll figure it out. And yes, they might not do it the way you would do it. But they might do it better.

Empowerment doesn't mean abandonment. It means presence without control. It means availability without interference. It means caring enough to let people fail and learn, rather than controlling enough to prevent thc failure and prevent the learning.

This is what I mean by trusting growth: you're trusting that people can develop. You're betting that the space you give them is more valuable than the control you maintain. You're accepting that the path they take might be messier than the path you would choose, but the destination and the person who arrives there will be better.

What Empowerment Requires

Empowerment isn't possible without the things we've discussed throughout this book.

It requires trust. You have to believe that people can figure it out. Not in theory. Actually, believe it. And they have to know you believe it.

It requires psychological safety. People need to know that if they stumble, if they try something and it doesn't work, the response will be learning, not punishment. They need to know that failure in service of growth is acceptable.

It requires maturity. You have to know when to step in and when to stay back. When to provide guidance and when to let someone learn the hard way. When to protect them from unnecessary chaos and when to let them face the challenge that will grow them.

It requires empathy. You have to understand what that person needs to grow. What they're ready for. What will challenge them without breaking them. You have to see them as individuals, not as resources.

It requires courage. It takes courage to let go. It takes courage to watch someone struggle when you could solve it yourself. It takes courage to accept that they might fail. It takes courage to believe that the growth is worth the risk.

Without these things—trust, psychological safety, maturity, empathy, courage—empowerment becomes recklessness. It becomes abandonment. It becomes throwing people in the deep end and hoping they can swim.

But with these things? With these things, empowerment becomes the most powerful leadership tool that exists.

The Bandwidth Question

Here's something else that empowerment gives you: bandwidth.

When you're micromanaging—when you're overseeing every decision, checking every step, maintaining visibility and control—you're consumed by the details. You're in the weeds. You're reactive. You're solving immediate problems.

You're also completely consumed. You have no bandwidth for strategy. No bandwidth for vision. No bandwidth for the larger picture.

But when you empower your team, something shifts. You're no longer consumed by day-to-day execution. Your people are handling that. Your job becomes different—you're setting direction, removing obstacles, developing people, thinking about the future.

You get bandwidth. You get space. You get the ability to focus on larger strategies and vision.

And here's the thing: that's actually where you should be. That's where your value is. Not in executing tasks—your team can do that. Your value is in seeing where the organization needs to go, in thinking about what comes next, in building capability for the future.

Micromanagement trades your highest value work for your lowest value work. It trades strategy for task management. It trades vision for control.

Empowerment lets you do what you actually should be doing: leading.

The Philosophy at the Heart of This Book

If I had to distil everything I've learned over 25 years into a single philosophy, it would be this:

Leadership is about creating conditions where people can do their best work and become better versions of themselves.

Not about controlling people. Not about managing tasks. Not about protecting yourself. Not about projecting yourself as the hero.

Leadership is about creating conditions.

That means:

- Creating psychological safety so people can be honest
- Building trust so people can take risks
- Providing clarity so people know what matters
- Removing obstacles so people can focus
- Empowering people so they can own their work
- Protecting people so they can grow
- Developing people so they can handle greater challenges
- Standing for people so they know they're valued

Everything in this book—every insight, every chapter, every story—is in service of creating those conditions.

And at the center of all of it is empowerment. Because empowerment is what allows all of these other things to actually work.

The Integration

Let me connect the dots. Show how empowerment integrates with everything else you've read.

When Potential Meets Setbacks (Chapter 16): You're empowering someone by giving them space to try a different project, to work with a different mentor, to figure out how to apply their capability in a new context.

Speak Up (Chapter 22): Psychological safety enables empowerment. People can't take ownership if they're afraid of the consequences of failure.

When Do You Give Up? (Chapter 13): Sometimes empowerment means letting someone keep trying when the easy thing would be to give up on them. Trusting their growth.

The Efficiency Illusion (Chapter 21): Empowerment means letting teams experiment with how they work, rather than dictating processes from above. It means trusting that frontline teams know better than executives.

Captain on the Bridge (Chapter 23): The captain trusts the crew. That's empowerment. Kirk doesn't micromanage Spock. He sets direction and lets Spock execute.

From Burnout to Breakthrough (Chapter 14): The Executive MBA worked because it gave the leader space to rediscover purpose. Empowerment is giving people space to grow, even when it costs in the short term.

The Ego Trap (Chapter 15): Micromanagement often comes from ego—the need to be right, to be in control, to be seen as the one who has all the answers. Empowerment requires letting go of that.

Motivation in Uncertain Times (Chapter 25): In the pandemic, teams that thrived were the ones that were empowered to figure out how to work remotely. The control-oriented teams struggled.

Leadership Is Protection, Not Projection (Chapter 27): Protecting your team means empowering them. Giving them the space and support to do their best work.

Every chapter, every insight, points toward the same thing: that leadership works when you empower people. That organizations thrive when they trust people to figure it out.

What Empowerment Actually Costs

I want to be clear about this: empowerment has costs. Real costs.

It costs control. You have to accept that you don't know exactly what's happening at every moment. That people might make decisions you wouldn't make. That the path might be different from the path you would choose.

It costs in the short term. Yes, they might stumble. Yes, it might take longer. Yes, the quality might not be perfect in the early attempts. You have to accept that short-term inefficiency is the price of long-term capability.

It costs emotionally. It's hard to watch someone struggle when you could solve it yourself. It's hard to let go. It's hard to trust.

It costs politically, sometimes. In organizations where control is valued, where visibility is seen as a proxy for work, empowerment can make you look less busy. Your team is doing the work; you're not visibly working. That can hurt in some environments.

But the cost of micromanagement is higher. It's the cost of people leaving. The cost of initiative dying. The cost of creativity being replaced with compliance. The cost of people doing exactly what they're told and nothing more. The cost of never discovering what people could actually do.

Empowerment has costs. But micromanagement has bigger costs.

The Question at the Center of Everything

Here's the question I've asked myself throughout my career:

Am I building capability or consuming it?

Micromanagement consumes capability. It uses people as resources—you extract work from them, but you don't develop them. Over time, your best people leave. You're left with people who've learned to do exactly what they're told.

Empowerment builds capability. It develops people. It grows their skills. It increases their confidence. It expands what they're capable of handling.

Every decision I make, I try to ask that question: Is this consuming capability or building it?

If I take over a decision that someone could make themselves, I'm consuming capability. I'm teaching them they're not capable of making decisions. I'm saying that my judgment is what matters.

If I step back and let them make it—with support, with guidance, but ultimately their decision—I'm building capability. I'm saying: I believe you can figure this out. I trust you.

Over time, the cumulative impact of those decisions is massive. It's the difference between a team that's become more capable and a team that's become dependent.

For Leaders Reading This

As you close this book, here's what I want you to take with you:

You don't have to be right about every decision. Your job isn't to have all the answers. Your job is to create conditions where good thinking can happen and good decisions can emerge.

Your team is more capable than you think. People will surprise you if you give them space. They'll figure things out you didn't expect them to figure out. They'll grow in ways you didn't anticipate.

Short-term inefficiency is the price of long-term capability. Yes, it's faster if you do it yourself. But you're not building a team that can operate without you. You're building a team that's dependent on you.

Empowerment doesn't mean abandonment. You're still there. You're still supporting. You're still removing obstacles. You're just doing it without the control. You're doing it with trust.

The people who will follow you across organizations, who will recommend you as a leader, who will work harder for you than for anyone else—they're the ones you empowered. Not the ones you controlled. Not the ones you managed closely. The ones you trusted.

Your highest value work is strategy and vision, not task execution. Get out of the weeds. Empower your team to handle the weeds. Focus on where the organization needs to go.

Culture is built through empowerment. The organizations where people do their best work, where they stay, where they grow—they're the organizations where people feel empowered. Where they have ownership. Where they're trusted.

The Simplicity at the Heart of Complexity

We've covered a lot in this book. 27 chapters. 33 insights. Dozens of stories and principles and frameworks.

But it all comes down to something simple: Do you trust people or do you control them?

Do you believe people want to do good work, or do you believe they need to be managed?

Do you believe people can figure it out, or do you believe you need to have all the answers?

Do you believe in empowerment or micromanagement?

Because your answer to that question determines everything else. It determines the culture you build. The people who stay and the people who leave. The results you get in the short term and the capability you build for the long term. The organization you create.

The Final Synthesis: Trust, Maturity, Empathy, and Courage

Let me bring it back to what this chapter promises: trust, maturity, empathy, and courage.

Trust: You have to trust that people are capable. That they want to do good work. That given the space, they'll figure it out. Trust is the foundation of empowerment. Without it, you'll always hold back. You'll always try to control.

Maturity: You have to know when to step in and when to step back. When to provide guidance and when to let someone learn the hard way. When to protect and when to expose them to challenge. Maturity is knowing the difference.

Empathy: You have to understand what each person needs. What they're ready for. What will develop them versus what will break them. Empathy is seeing the person, not just the role.

Courage: It takes courage to let go. It takes courage to believe in people when they're struggling. It takes courage to step back and let them figure it out. It takes courage to risk that they might fail. Courage is the thing that makes empowerment actually happen.

These four things—trust, maturity, empathy, and courage—they're not separate from empowerment. They're the foundation of it. They're what makes empowerment possible.

And if you develop these in yourself as a leader, empowerment will follow. It won't be a program you implement. It will be a way you lead.

The Invitation to You

This book has been my attempt to capture what I've learned over 25 years of leadership. The good decisions and the bad ones. The wins and the failures. The insights that came from experience and from the incredible people I've worked with.

But now it's your turn. The question isn't whether you agree with everything in this book. The question is: what will you do with it?

Which insights resonate? Which ones challenge you? Where do you feel called to lead differently?

And most importantly: will you empower people? Will you trust them? Will you create conditions where they can do their best work and become better versions of themselves?

That's the work. That's leadership.

Where We End Is Where We Begin

We started this book with fundamental questions about leadership. What does it actually mean to lead? What separates leaders who build something real from leaders who just manage what exists?

The answer, I believe, is empowerment.

It's the choice to trust instead of control. To develop instead of consume. To stand for instead of hide behind. To protect instead of project.

It's a choice you make every day. In every conversation. In every decision. In every moment where you could take over or step back.

The organizations that thrive are built by leaders who consistently choose empowerment. Who trusts their people. Who builds capability. Who create conditions where excellence is possible.

Those leaders are rare. They're valuable. They're needed.

Maybe you're one of them. Maybe you want to be.

If you do, here's your path: Trust. Develop maturity. Practice empathy. Gather courage.

And then empower. Every day. In every way you can.

That's where real leadership begins.

A Final Word

Thank you for taking this journey with me. For reading about persistence and humility, about innovation and governance, about protection and empowerment. For considering the insights I've tried to share.

The work of leadership is hard. It requires constantly choosing the harder path—the path that builds capability, that trusts people, that stands for others, that protects without controlling.

But it's also the most rewarding work there is. Because you get to see people grow. You get to build something real. You get to create an environment where excellence is possible.

That's leadership. That's what makes it worth doing.

Now go build something great. And remember: empower your people. Trust them. Stand for them. Protect them.

Everything else will follow.

Epilogue
Leadership Isn't a Designation – It's a Practice

What Leadership Actually Is

You've read 28 chapters. 33 insights. Dozens of stories about persistence and ego, about burnout and breakthrough, about governance and innovation, about risk and trust, about empowerment and protection.

But if you strip away all of that—if you reduce everything to its absolute essence—leadership is this:

A daily practice of trust, protection, empowerment, courage, and empathy.

Not a position you hold. Not a title on your business card. Not a level you've reached on the organizational hierarchy.

A practice. Something you do. Every day. Over and over. Getting better at it. Failing at it. Learning from the failure. Trying again.

The Daily Choice

Leadership isn't something that happens once. It's not a decision you make and then you're done. It's a series of choices you make throughout each day.

When a team member brings you a problem: Do you solve it for them or help them solve it? Do you project your expertise or do you protect their growth?

When something goes wrong: Do you distance yourself or do you step forward? Do you deflect blame or do you own the outcome?

When someone challenges your thinking: Do you defend your position or do you listen? Do you need to be right or do you need to get to the right answer?

When your team is discouraged: Do you hide the challenges or do you face them together? Do you project confidence or do you build trust through honesty?

When you don't know the answer: Do you pretend or do you admit it? Do you project certainty or do you model curiosity?

Each of these moments—and there are hundreds of them in every week—is where leadership actually happens. Not in the big speeches. Not in the strategic plans. Not in the org charts.

In the moments when you choose.

The Integration

Everything in this book connects to this daily practice.

Trust means choosing to believe that people are capable, even when they're struggling. It means betting on their growth instead of controlling their work.

Protection means choosing to stand for your team, even when it costs you. Even when they disappoint you. Even when it would be easier to protect yourself.

Empowerment means choosing to give people space, even when you could do it faster yourself. Even when you're not sure they can figure it out.

Courage means choosing to act even when you're uncertain. To let go even when you want to control. To be honest even when it's uncomfortable. To stand for people even when it's risky.

Empathy means choosing to see people as whole human beings, not as resources or problems to solve. To understand what they need, not just what the organization needs from them.

These aren't things you do once and then you've mastered leadership. They're things you practice. Every day. In every interaction. With every person.

And some days you'll do it well. Some days you'll fail. Some days you'll get halfway through a conversation before you realize you stopped listening and started defending.

That's practice. That's what practice looks like.

The Circles, Not the Ladder

Leadership isn't a climb. It's not about reaching some final destination where you've arrived, where you've figured it out, where you no longer have to work at it.

Leadership is circles. You return to the same principles at different levels, in different contexts, with different people, at different phases of your career.

Early in your career, you might practice empowerment by giving a team member a project to own. Later, you practice it by giving a department autonomy over their strategy. Later still, you practice it by trusting your entire organization to figure out how to implement a transformation.

The principle is the same. The scale changes.

You'll return to the question of ego again and again. You'll face the tension between short-term results and long-term health again and again. You'll encounter the choice between **loyalty** and competence again and again. You'll be tempted to hide behind your people instead of standing for them again and again.

Each time you face it, you have the opportunity to practice better. To understand it more deeply. To live it more fully.

That's not failure. That's mastery. Mastery is returning to the same thing and doing it better each time. It's not finishing the practice. It's deepening it.

The Ripple Effect

Here's what you need to understand about practicing leadership this way:

It spreads.

When you stand for your people, they learn to stand for the people they lead. When you create psychological safety, the people you develop create it in their teams. When you empower people, they empower others. When you practice protection and empathy and courage, you're modelling it.

And those people do the same with the people they lead.

You're not just building a team. You're building a culture. You're not just changing how one department works. You're changing how the organization works.

The leaders you develop will develop other leaders. The culture you build will spread through the organization. The practice you live will be replicated by dozens of people who learned from you.

That's how real change happens. Not through mandates from above. Not through reorganizations and restructurings. But through leaders who, day after day, choose to practice something different.

Who choose trust instead of control. Protection instead of projection. Empowerment instead of micromanagement. Courage instead of safety. Empathy instead of efficiency.

The Cost and the Reward

I won't pretend this practice is easy. It costs something.

It costs control. It costs certainty. It costs the ability to hide behind systems and processes. It costs the comfort of doing things the way they've always been done.

It costs emotionally. It requires vulnerability. It requires admitting when you don't know. It requires letting people you care about struggle when you could solve it for them. It requires taking risks.

It costs politically, sometimes. In organizations that reward command-and-control leadership, this practice can make you look soft. It can slow you down. It can make you less visible, because your team is doing the work instead of you.

But the reward is immeasurable.

You build teams where people actually want to work. Where people care. Where people go the extra mile not because they're afraid but because they're inspired. Where people stay not because they have to but because they want to.

You build cultures where excellence is possible. Where innovation happens. Where problems get surfaced instead of hidden. Where people do their best work because they trust their leader and themselves.

You build something real. Something that lasts. Something that matters beyond the quarter, beyond the year, beyond your tenure in a role.

And when you leave—when you move on, when you get promoted, when you retire—the culture you built remains. The people you developed carry it forward. The practice spreads.

That's the reward. That's why it's worth the cost.

Power and Politics

You might have noticed something missing from these 28 chapters: I haven't spent much time on power dynamics and organizational politics.

That's deliberate.

Not because they don't exist. They do. In every organization. At every level.

But because I believe how you approach them defines the kind of leader you become.

Understanding Power Without Surrendering to It

Here's my stance: You need to understand power dynamics. You need to see them, recognize them, read the room, understand who holds influence and why.

But understanding them is not the same as surrendering to them.

Just because someone is powerful doesn't mean they're right. Just because the politics point in one direction doesn't mean that's where you should go. Just because it's easier to submit to the all-powerful doesn't mean you should.

You must be strong enough to absorb the pressure and push back when you feel strongly about your stand. Not recklessly. Not naively. But with eyes wide open about what you're doing and why it matters.

That takes courage. Real courage. The kind that says, "I see the power dynamics, I understand the risk, and I'm choosing to stand for what I believe is right anyway."

The Politics Game

I've never been a big fan of organizational politics. I think it's largely a waste of time and effort—energy that could be spent building something real instead of manoeuvring through manufactured complexity.

But here's the reality: if you cannot manoeuvre around politics, you will succumb to them. They'll suffocate your impact. They'll drain your energy. They'll force you into a game you never wanted to play.

So, what's the answer?

My way has been to work cutting through politics without fear of consequence. Not to play the game better, but to work so directly, so transparently, so focused on the mission that the politics become less relevant.

If you're victorious, you live to fight another day. Your directness becomes your reputation. People learn that you won't play the games, and sometimes—not always, but sometimes—that earns respect.

If you succumb to it, if the politics win, then I accept and move on. I don't dwell on it. I don't become bitter. I don't start playing the game I said I wouldn't play.

Because the moment you compromise on this—the moment you decide to "just play the game a little bit"—you've already lost something more important than any political victory.

The Line You Draw

This isn't about being naive. It's not about ignoring reality or pretending power dynamics don't matter.

It's about drawing a line for yourself.

On one side of that line: understanding the landscape, being strategic, picking your battles, knowing when to push and when to wait.

On the other side: compromising your principles, protecting yourself at others' expense, playing politics instead of building something real, surrendering to power just because it's power.

You get to decide where that line is. You get to decide what you'll stand for and what you won't tolerate.

But once you've decided, you have to live it. Consistently. Even when it costs you.

That's part of the practice too.

The Question

As you close this book, I want to leave you with one question:

What will you do tomorrow that's different?

Not next month when you've had time to think about it. Not when you get promoted to a position where you can implement these ideas. Tomorrow.

Will you have a conversation with someone on your team where you listen instead of directing? Will you let someone own a decision instead of approving it? Will you admit something you don't know instead of pretending you do? Will you stand for someone instead of protecting yourself? Will you create space for someone to fail and learn instead of stepping in?

Will you practice?

Because leadership isn't about knowing these things. It's about doing them. It's not about agreeing with this book. It's about changing how you show up tomorrow.

That's where leadership actually lives. Not in understanding. In practice.

The Beginning

This book is not the end. It's not a destination you've reached by reading it. It's a beginning. It's an invitation to a different way of leading.

The work starts now. Tomorrow. In the next conversation you have. In the next decision you make. In the next moment when you have to choose between protecting yourself and standing for your people.

That's where real leadership happens. In those moments. In that practice. Day after day. For the rest of your career.

Leadership isn't a position. It's not a title. It's not something you achieve and then you're done.

Leadership is a practice. A daily choice. A way of showing up with trust, protection, empowerment, courage, and empathy.

It's showing up that way when it's easy. And especially when it's hard.

That's what separates leaders who build something real from leaders who just manage what exists.

That's what makes leadership worth doing.

Now go practice. Your team is waiting. Your organization is waiting. The people you'll develop are waiting.

The work of leadership isn't in the office. It's in the choices you make every single day.

Make them count

About the Author

Liyakhat Ali Khan is a seasoned R&D engineering leader with over 25 years of experience driving innovation and building high-performance teams in the global automotive industry. His last role as a Senior Program Manager at Mercedes Benz R&D India and Daimler Truck Innovation Center India (DTICI), he had been instrumental in establishing and scaling new R&D capabilities from the ground up, leading complex cross-border programs across Germany, Japan, and the United States.

He holds a Bachelor of Engineering (Mechanical) from the prestigious University Visvesvaraya College of Engineering, Bangalore, and an MBA(E) from Symbiosis Institute of Management Studies, Pune—a combination that uniquely positions him at the intersection of technical excellence and business leadership.

His career has been defined by a unique blend of startup agility and enterprise-level execution. With rich experience across both OEM and Tier-1 supplier organizations, he has had the privilege of working alongside domestic and international leaders, gaining diverse perspectives on leadership and innovation across the automotive value chain. Specializing in automotive interiors and exteriors—particularly interior systems engineering and cockpit modules—he has led multi-disciplinary teams through the entire product development lifecycle, from concept to Start of Production (SOP). His leadership approach combines technical depth with strategic vision, enabling teams to deliver innovative, cost-optimized solutions in fast-paced, matrix environments.

A recognized innovator, he holds multiple patents in automotive interior systems and has received numerous internal awards and recognitions for excellence in program execution, innovation, and team leadership. His contributions have consistently delivered value to organizations while advancing technical capabilities in the industry.

Throughout his career, he has championed the principles explored in this book: building trust within teams, fostering cross-cultural collaboration, balancing strategic thinking with hands-on execution, and creating environments where innovation and people development go hand in hand.

When he's not leading R&D programs or mentoring emerging leaders, he continues to explore how technical excellence and human-centered leadership can drive transformational change in complex organizations.

He is based in Pune, India.

Connect:

LinkedIn: www.linkedin.com/in/liyakhat-ali-khan